To Laura, Giorgio, Riccardo and Alberto

Giuseppe's Easy Bakes

Sweet Italian Treats

GIUSEPPE DELL'ANNO

Photography by Matt Russell

Hardie Grant

QUADRILLE

INTRODUCTION
6

CAKES
22

CAKELETS
58

BISCUITS & COOKIES
90

SWEET TREATS
142

SAUCES
170

INDEX (INCLUDING INDEXES FOR DAIRY-FREE,
EGG-FREE, NUT-FREE, GLUTEN-FREE RECIPES)
182

THANKS
190

INTRO
DUCTION

WHAT'S IN THIS BOOK, AND WHAT IS NOT

Italian baking masterpieces, the likes of panettone or pandoro, are not always easy to make at home. Their exceptional level of flavour and texture demands a skillset that even the best bakers take years to master. Also, delicacies like Sicilian cannoli, albeit much easier to make, will still require at the very least some forward planning. No doubt it is all for a good cause: those heavenly yeasted doughs and elaborate multi-texture desserts are hard to beat for the big occasions!

However, when I set out to write this book, I decided to focus on simple, more rustic bakes instead, those that my dad, a professional chef and a passionate baker, would sometime prepare for the family with less than one hour's notice, and with whatever ingredients were available in our cupboard.

My ultimate ambition is to enable everybody, including those with little or no baking experience, to produce good cakes, well-made biscuits and delectable treats without too much effort or time-dedication. Simple, robust recipes that work are key to this, even though, in the baking world, simplicity is often underrated. Perhaps you can consider this book almost as an antidote to the baking madness that all too often floods our social channels these days, an escape from architectural bakes, hyper-decorated fondant, or cakes that defy the laws of physics...

You will not find exotic methods or professional techniques in these pages; even piping and decorating have been reduced to a minimum. Instead, these recipes have been handpicked for their deliciousness and simplicity, to provide you with tempting flavour combinations – of course, unapologetically Italian – in a set of simple and accessible bakes. To simplify things further, those steps that are more easily shown than described have been filmed, and the videos are linked to the recipe through QR codes, allowing you to access the tutorials on your smartphone in just one tap.

But simple does not mean bland and rustic does not mean ugly! The exceptional flavour and pretty looks of these bakes not only have passed the test of time (some date as far back as the fourteenth century), but still grant them centre stage in modern Italian baking, and prime estate in the windows of coffee shops all over the country.

I genuinely hope that these recipes will not only add the all-important wow factor to your celebrations, but will make your elevenses sweeter, fill the kids' mid-afternoon snack with mouth-watering cakes, and populate your daily coffee-breaks with the tastiest dunking biscuits.

HOW TO USE THIS BOOK

I have organized the recipes in this book into chapters by size and type, beginning with simple cakes and tarts for slicing and sharing, followed by individual cakelets, biscuits and cookies, then sweet treats to make in advance that offer an indulgent nibble.

Each recipe has a summary box, with an estimate of the preparation and baking time, and its suitability to most dietary needs. Recipes that make use of raw or partially cooked eggs are identified as such, for the sake of those with a weak or compromised immune system.

None of the cakes in this book involves complicated fillings or extravagant coatings: most are intended as tasty midweek treats, ready to serve shortly after baking. However, for those occasions that do call for a little extra, the final chapter provides a selection of pourable sauces, matched to the main flavour of your bake, that will easily elevate your cake to the status of sophisticated dessert.

Whatever you choose to bake, I recommend you read my comments here on equipment and measuring – all in the interest of making your time and effort spent an entirely pleasurable experience.

Tinware

Even the simplest cake can be elevated by a fancy tin, and I often rely on the mesmerizing geometries of the Nordic Ware collections (nordicware.com) to add a touch of effortless sculptural flair to my bakes. These tins, as any other good-quality mould, require little preparation: if you have any available, a light coating of cake release spray is often enough to guarantee successful unmoulding every time. Otherwise, generously smear the inside with butter, then dust it with flour, tapping off any excess. For any mould with a lot of detail, this is easiest done by chilling it in the fridge first, then brushing melted butter inside using a pastry brush before dusting it with flour. Replace butter with vegetable spread for dairy-free bakes, and flour with cornflour (cornstarch) in gluten-free recipes.

The bundt tins that I have used in this book are all 24cm (9½in) diameter and 2.5 litre (87fl oz) capacity, and can be replaced by a conventional 23cm (9in) springform tin. Baking times will change slightly with the size, shape and brand of the tin, so always perform the skewer test before taking the cake out of the oven. This is done by inserting a long skewer (or a toothpick) all the way to the bottom in the deepest part the cake. When the skewer comes out clean and dry, the cake is ready. Perform this test as quickly as possible, ideally while the cake is still in the oven: one of the most common mistakes is to keep the oven door open for an unnecessarily long time while checking the cake: this reduces its temperature significantly, potentially jeopardizing the bake.

Ovens

I bake using an electric oven and all oven temperatures in this book refer to 'static', or 'conventional' setting. This is when two heating elements, one at the top and one at the bottom of the oven chamber, heat up. If you have to bake on 'fan' setting, also known as 'forced air' or 'convection', then lower the temperature stated in the recipe by 15–20 degrees and keep a closer eye on the bake. Needless to say, all ovens are different so the baking times can only be considered indicative: use your senses and assess when the cake is ready with the tests and clues included in the recipes.

A few recipes make enough items to fill two baking trays: I recommend baking these individually for an even, more controlled bake. Allegedly, fan ovens can bake two trays at once, but I am always disappointed with the result, as I often end up with some items underbaked and some overbaked.

Recipes that use a microwave oven, typically for melting butter or chocolate, refer to a conventional 800W appliance. Microwaves with much higher wattage are common nowadays: for those, the timing should be reduced accordingly.

THE SECRET TO SUCCESSFUL BAKES? WEIGH EVERYTHING, ALWAYS!

Baking is not all about accuracy, but successful baking is. My ingredient ratios have been worked out carefully and the recipes relentlessly tested using gram weight, not cups. This is because the weight of one cup of flour can vary by as much as 40% depending on how tightly it is packed. Different sugars vary too, according to crystal size, and while a cup of unsifted icing (confectioner's) sugar weighs 140g, just 115g of sifted icing sugar will fill the same cup measure. Not even the most robust recipe can make up for these variations in volume. You simply stand a much better chance of producing a flawless bake if you weigh your ingredients carefully; volumetric measures like cups are not precise enough, and I recommend you use a set of digital scales that are accurate to the gram. The only exceptions are teaspoons and tablespoons as the quantities are small and unlikely to compromise your bake. Always use measuring spoons rather than table cutlery and keep the measurements consistent by levelling the top of dry ingredients using the back of a knife.

Nevertheless, I did include cup measurements in my recipes for those that do not have easy access to a reliable set of kitchen scales; the table below summarizes the cup-to-gram conversions used throughout the book for the most common ingredients:

1 cup of soft wheat 00 flour or plain (all-purpose) flour = 140g
1 cup of cornflour (cornstarch) = about 100g
1 cup of chestnut flour = 140g
1 cup of semolina = 180g
1 cup of caster (superfine) sugar = scant 200g (see page 16)
1 cup of unsifted icing (confectioner's) sugar = 140g
1 cup of dark or light brown soft sugar = 200g
1 cup of clear honey = about 280g
1 cup of cocoa powder = about 100g
1 cup of butter = 225g
scant 1 cup of vegetable oil = 200g
1 cup of semi-skimmed milk = 240g
1 cup of cream = about 215g (single/whipping); about 255g
    (double/heavy)
1 cup of ricotta = about 225g
1 cup of mascarpone = scant 200g
1 cup of natural whole yogurt = about 215g
1 cup of Greek yogurt = about 200g
1 cup of whole almonds = about 130g
1 cup of ground almonds = 100g

I recommend you weigh your eggs too because, although their size is often defined by local food authorities, it is only approximate and it may vary significantly. All my recipes refer to the weight of eggs without the shell. As a general rule, I call an egg 'medium' when it weighs 50g and 'large' when it weighs 60g. However, when following a recipe, do not go by the number of eggs, instead beat them in a spouted jug and pour only the weight required in your mixture.

*I opt for caster sugar in all my recipes – its fine crystals make it quicker to cream or dissolve. Caster can be substituted with granulated sugar but, because of the small weight-to-volume difference between the two, I always advocate measuring using scales, not cups. It may only be a few grams, but as you scale up the amounts, that difference will affect the sweetness of your bakes.

MY (FEW) WONDER INGREDIENTS

In the making of this book, I have actively avoided the use of any exotic or extravagant ingredient: my ideal bake is one that can be done with cupboard staples or that requires minimal ad hoc shopping. However, there are a couple of ingredients that come up often in my recipes and that are absolutely worth resourcing: you will find useful links to distributors and online shops on giuseppedellanno.com.

Unwaxed organic citrus fruits

Very few recipes of mine do not call for some form of citrus flavour, often added with either the zest or the peel of the fruit. The freshness and tanginess they provide is simply unbeatable!

Although safe to eat, the range of chemicals that supermarket fruits are sprayed with does not make them my favourite choice when it comes to eating their skin. Common sense suggests that going for the least-treated option available is best.

Nothing beats untreated fruit picked fresh from your garden, but few of us have that luxury, so unwaxed organic fruits remain the next best thing. However, if you struggle to source them, you can batch-unwax conventional supermarket fruit easily: place them in a colander (strainer) and slowly pour freshly boiled water from a kettle over them. This will melt and displace most of the wax. Then rinse them under cold water and scrub them with a clean brush to remove any leftover residue.

Amarena cherries

Amarena cherries are semi-candied sour cherries, sold in their sugary, deep-purple syrup; the special processing method preserves their plumpness and gives them a distinctively sweet and acidic taste. They must not be confused with conventional glacé cherries, which are fully candied instead, and therefore drier, harder and without much of their cherry flavour left.

Amarena cherries in syrup were first commercialized over a century ago in Italy by Fabbri (en.fabbri1905.com). The company is still family-owned today and distributes its cherries in iconic blue-patterned jars. I am undeniably and unapologetically a big fan: they are an extremely versatile ingredient that adds bursts of flavour to even the simplest of desserts. Just a spoonful liberally drizzled over yogurt or vanilla ice cream will get you hooked in no time.

The flavour and texture of amarena cherries are quite unique and cannot be replaced easily with fresh or frozen cherries. However, they are easily sourced through online retailers and specialist shops: head to my website for a list of links to distributors: giuseppedellanno.com

Soft wheat oo flour

A must-have ingredient in Italian baking, and one that the vast majority of my recipes calls for, is soft wheat 00 flour. This grade is ideal for sweet bakes as its low protein content delivers sponges with exceptional softness and biscuits with unbeatable crumbliness. The bran-free and extra-refined particles ensure bakes with a very fine crumb and pastries with a professional-level texture.

Soft wheat 00 flour is relatively easy to find in large supermarkets, or can be sourced through online retailers; head to my website for a list of common suppliers. Sometimes it is marketed as 'sponge flour', but be careful to avoid any mix that contains additional baking powder: none of my recipes uses self-raising flour as I like to control the amount of leavening agent that goes into each bake.

Plain (all-purpose) flour can be used as an alternative if soft wheat 00 flour is not available: when choosing it, check the nutritional information on the back of the pack and go for a flour that contains 10g or less proteins per 100g of product.

Pisto

Pisto is a very aromatic blend of ground spices featuring regularly in Neapolitan bakes: I always have a jar in my pantry as I like to add a pinch even to simple shortbread to add extra warmth. Ready-made pisto is not easy to source outside of Italy, but it can be made at home in less than 10 minutes. The must-have spices are cinnamon, coriander seeds, cloves and nutmeg, but my version – used in my family ever since I can remember – also includes star anise and black pepper, which give it extra depth and a little heat.

Traditionally, pisto is made by grinding the spices to a fine powder in a pestle and mortar (the word literally means 'beaten'); however, an electric mill makes the job effortless. Just make sure that the mill is stopped as soon as possible to avoid overheating the spices: it should not take more than 30 seconds at high speed. Resist the temptation to use ready-ground spices, if you can: using whole ingredients makes a noticeable difference to the overall scent of the blend, and it is definitely worth the extra effort. The amounts below will make about 30g (1oz): it is more than you need for a single bake, but it can be stored in an airtight jar for several months without losing much flavour.

15g (½oz) cinnamon sticks (about 4 sticks, 8cm/3¼in each),
    chopped into 2cm (¾in) chunks
4g (about 2 tsp) black peppercorns
2g (about 1 tsp) whole cloves
2g (about 1 tsp) coriander seeds
2g (about 2 small pods) star anise
5g nutmeg (about 5 tsp freshly grated nutmeg)

Place the cinnamon sticks, peppercorns, cloves, coriander seeds and star anise in a mortar and grind using the pestle to a fine powder. Using pressing and swirling actions rather than pounding works best and makes the job shorter. Grate the nutmeg and add it to the blend, mixing until fully combined.

CAKES

Torta di mele della nonna	24
Torta all'uva nera	26
Torta caffè corretto	28
Pan di pesca	30
Torta frutti rossi e ricotta	32
Torta al mandarino	34
Torta ubriaca	36
Torta alle noci	38
Ciambellone di Pasqua	40
Migliaccio	42
Strudel pere e prugne	44
Cheesecake caffè e amaretti	48
Torta di datteri	50
Torta cocco e amarena	52
Sbriciolata alle ciliegie	54
Cuor di Sicilia	56

Grandma's apple cake

Few things epitomize timeless home baking like the intoxicating scent of a warm apple cake. My recipe has been tried and tested for generations and it never fails to deliver. The sponge is delicately flavoured by the balanced use of spices and the texture is substantial enough to hold up a generous helping of fruit, while remaining pleasantly soft thanks to the cunning addition of mascarpone.

There is no need to be picky with the type of apple: I prefer sweeter, crunchier varieties like Gala or Golden Delicious and try to avoid ones that are too soft or watery, but this cake can be baked with whatever apples you have at home.

The joy of this cake is that it ages beautifully: in fact, it is better the day after, when the juices from the fruit have had time to infuse the sponge. Classically served with a scoop of vanilla ice cream, it goes exceptionally well with a drizzle of yogurt sauce (page 173) or caramel sauce (page 181).

SERVES up to 12

for a 23cm (9in) springform cake tin

zest of 1 unwaxed organic lemon
50g (3 tbsp plus 1 tsp) freshly squeezed lemon juice
600g (1lb 5oz) sweet apples (about 3 large or 4 medium fruits)
100g (scant ½ cup) unsalted butter, plus extra for greasing
200g (7oz) egg (about 4 medium eggs), at room temperature
180g (scant ¾ cup) light brown soft sugar
1 tsp vanilla bean paste
⅛ tsp salt
100g (scant ½ cup) mascarpone
250g (1¾ cups plus 2 tbsp) soft wheat 00 flour or plain (all-purpose) flour
2 tsp baking powder
2 tsp ground cinnamon
¼ tsp ground cloves
2 tbsp caster (superfine) sugar
60g (2¼oz) apricot or peach jam (preserve) for brushing

1. Grease the tin and line the base with baking paper. Set the shelf in the lower half of the oven and preheat it to 180°C/350°F/Gas mark 4.
2. Put the lemon zest and juice in a medium bowl. Wash and pat dry the apples, set one aside for later and, without peeling, dice the rest in 1cm (½in) pieces, discarding the cores. Add the diced apples to the bowl with the zest and juice, stir to coat the apple thoroughly, and set aside.
3. Put the butter in a small microwave-safe bowl and melt it: 40 seconds in the microwave should be enough. Set aside to cool.
4. Put the eggs, brown sugar, vanilla and salt in the bowl of a stand mixer and whisk on high speed until pale and frothy. It will take about 5 minutes. With the mixer going, trickle in the melted butter. Add the mascarpone and whisk for a further minute to incorporate it fully.
5. Take the bowl off the stand and sift in the flour, baking powder, cinnamon and cloves then fold them in with a silicone spatula until no clumps of flour are visible. Add the diced apples with their juices and fold them in until fully incorporated. Pour the batter into the prepared tin and level it out with the spatula. Core then slice the remaining apple into thin wedges and arrange the slices on top of the cake in a sunburst pattern. Sprinkle the cake with caster sugar and bake for about 1 hour or until the top is a deep caramel colour and a skewer inserted in the centre of the cake comes out clean.
6. Take the cake out of the oven and let it cool for 5 minutes. Meanwhile, warm the jam in the microwave for 20–30 seconds then brush it over the top of the cake. Allow to cool in the tin until just warm, then unmould onto a wire rack to finish cooling. Torta di mele della nonna keeps for up to a week under a cake dome.

PREP TIME: 25 minutes

TOTAL BAKING TIME: 1 hour

BAKING TEMPERATURE: 180°C/350°F/Gas mark 4

nut-free

TORTA ALL'UVA NERA

Black grape cake

Every bite of torta all'uva nera delivers bursts of sweet juiciness in a soft and fragrant crumb. The yogurt in the batter guarantees a pillowy structure and the generous helping of fresh grapes adds a delicate yet satisfying texture. If that was not enough, this cake is extremely simple to make: it will be in the oven in less than 20 minutes, leaving only a single bowl to wash up.

It is traditionally baked in late summer or early autumn, at the peak of the harvest, when grapes are abundant and at their sweetest. You can use your favourite variety, but there is something in the plump sweetness of black grapes that I find irresistible. Serve on its own for breakfast, brunch or afternoon tea; pair it with a scoop of ice cream for an elegant dessert.

SERVES up to 12

for a 23cm (9in) springform cake tin

butter, for greasing
400g (14oz) seedless black grapes
150g (5½oz) egg (about 3 medium eggs), at room temperature
170g (scant 1 cup) caster (superfine) sugar
1 tsp vanilla bean paste
⅛ tsp salt
100g (scant ½ cup) vegetable oil (preferably corn or sunflower)
160g (¾ cup) whole natural yogurt
200g (1½ cups) soft wheat 00 flour or plain (all-purpose) flour
50g (½ cup) cornflour (cornstarch)
1½ tsp baking powder
zest of 1 unwaxed organic lemon
icing (confectioner's) sugar, for dusting

1. Set the shelf in the lowest position of the oven and preheat it to 180°C/350°F/Gas mark 4. Grease the tin and line the base with baking paper. Wash the grapes, remove the stalks then drain and pat dry. Set aside.

2. Put the eggs, sugar, vanilla and salt in a bowl large enough to accommodate all the ingredients and whisk with a handheld electric whisk (or use a stand mixer) at high speed, until the sugar has completely dissolved and the mixture is pale and fluffy. It will take about 3–4 minutes. Still whisking, slowly trickle first the oil and then the yogurt into the bowl. Keep whisking for another minute until the liquids are fully incorporated.

3. Sift the flour, cornflour and baking powder into the bowl, then add the lemon zest. Whisk again at medium speed until the batter looks smooth. Add two-thirds of the grapes to the batter and fold them in, then pour the batter into the tin, level with a spatula or the back of a spoon and scatter the remaining grapes across the top. Bake for 48–50 minutes or until a skewer inserted in the deepest part of the cake comes out clean. Leave the cake in the tin to cool for a few minutes before transferring it to a wire rack to cool completely.

4. When ready to serve, transfer the cake to a serving plate and decorate with a dusting of icing sugar, using a 15cm (6in) plate in the centre of the cake as a stencil. It will keep for up to 3 days under a cake dome.

● nut-free   **PREP TIME:** 20 minutes   **TOTAL BAKING TIME:** 48–50 minutes   **BAKING TEMPERATURE:** 180°C/350°F/Gas mark 4

Cheeky coffee cake

Caffè corretto is a cheeky espresso served with an added dash of liqueur, typically grappa, sambuca or cognac. It is a rather welcome conclusion to an indulgent lunch, especially in the colder months. My grandmother would never forgo a drop of sambuca in her coffee on Christmas Day, and who can blame her?

Torta caffè corretto translates that perfect combination of coffee and liqueur into cake form, and blends it together with the nutty undertone of almonds. Dark rum lends this cake a spicier flavour, whereas sambuca gives it more of a sweeter kick: for an alcohol-free version, swap the liqueur for whole milk.

The flavour is intense but delicate, and the texture is pleasantly dense. The slices are robust enough to be dunked in caffè latte for breakfast or to be served with ice cream or fresh cream to end a meal. Coffee sauce (page 180 and milk chocolate sauce (page 173) both complement torta caffè corretto, but if you try it once with the caramel sauce (page 181), you will never serve it any other way!

SERVES up to 12

for a 24cm (9½in), 2.5-litre (87-fl oz) bundt tin or a 23cm (9in) springform cake tin

200g (¾ cup plus 2 tbsp) boiling water
2 tbsp instant coffee
160g (scant ¾ cup) unsalted butter, at room temperature and diced, plus extra for greasing
160g (5¾oz) egg (about 3 medium eggs), at room temperature
280g (1½ cups) dark brown soft sugar
⅛ tsp salt
1 tsp vanilla bean paste
100g (scant ½ cup) whipping (heavy) cream (35–40% fat)
350g (2⅔ cups) soft wheat 00 flour or plain (all-purpose) flour, plus extra for dusting
3 tsp baking powder
150g (1½ cups) ground almonds
50g (3 tbsp) dark rum or sambuca liqueur
icing (confectioner's) sugar, for dusting

1. Set the shelf in the lower half of the oven so that the top of the bundt tin sits just below mid-point. Preheat it to 160°C/320°F/Gas mark 3. Grease the tin with butter and dust it with flour, tapping off the excess.
2. Pour the boiling water in a medium bowl, dissolve the coffee and add the butter so that it melts in the hot coffee. Add the eggs, sugar, salt and vanilla to the bowl of a stand mixer and whisk until the mixture is pale and frothy; it will take about 6–8 minutes. With the whisk still going, slowly pour the cream into the eggs, followed by the coffee and butter mixture, and keep whisking until fully incorporated.
3. Take the bowl off the mixer and sift in the flour and baking powder. Very gently fold them into the batter, then add the ground almonds and gently fold these in too. Finally, add the liqueur and combine. Pour the batter into the tin and bake for 1 hour 10–15 minutes, or until a skewer inserted into the deepest part of the cake comes out clean.
4. Leave the cake to cool completely in the tin, then turn it out onto a serving plate and decorate with a light dusting of icing sugar. Serve at room temperature. Torta caffè corretto keeps for up to 3–4 days under a cake dome.

PREP TIME: 20 minutes

TOTAL BAKING TIME: 1 hour 10-15 minutes

BAKING TEMPERATURE: 160°C/320°F/Gas mark 3

PAN DI PESCA
Peach loaf

My Italian childhood summers smelled like peach: a bowl full of juicy, fragrant wedges of this glorious fruit was my daily mid-morning snack, eaten with bare, salty hands on the beach, between a swim and a dive. That intoxicating scent is so ingrained in my memory that, to this day, every bite of a ripe peach brings back images of bright, hot and sunny landscapes. No wonder pan di pesca is one of my favourite summer cakes: it is perfectly sweet, delicately flavoured and beautifully aromatic. If prepared with fresh nectarines, no peeling is needed. This recipe works best with ripe fruits, but it can also be made with canned peaches in the colder months.

The cake is also very easy to make: what better way to spend a summer afternoon with the kids than creating some indelible memories for them too? Serve at room temperature with mascarpone (page 175), yogurt (page 173) or strawberry sauce (page 180).

SERVES up to 14

for a 30 x 12cm (12 x 4½in) loaf tin, 1.5-litre (52fl oz) capacity

butter, for greasing
300g (10½oz) peaches, peeled and pitted (fresh or canned)
10g (⅓ oz) fresh mint sprigs
150g (5½oz) egg (about 3 medium eggs)
180g (1 cup) caster (superfine) sugar
1 tsp vanilla bean paste
⅛ tsp salt
100g (¼ cup plus 3 tbsp) vegetable oil (preferably corn or sunflower)
250g (1¾ cups plus 2 tbsp) soft wheat 00 flour or plain (all-purpose) flour
3 tsp baking powder
60g (3 tbsp) peach jam (preserve), for brushing

1. Set the shelf in the lowest position of the oven and preheat it to 180°C/350°F/Gas mark 4. Grease the tin and line it with baking paper.
2. Roughly chop 150g (5½oz) of the peaches, reserving the rest. Put the chopped pieces in the bowl of a food processor, add the mint then blitz to a pulp and set aside. Put the eggs, sugar, vanilla and salt in a bowl large enough to accommodate all the ingredients. Whisk the mixture at high speed with a handheld whisk (or use a stand mixer) until the sugar is completely dissolved and the mixture looks pale and frothy; it will take about 3–4 minutes.
3. With the whisk still going, slowly trickle the oil into the bowl, and whisk for a further minute. Add the peach pulp and whisk again to incorporate it. Sift the flour and baking powder into the bowl and whisk one last time at minimum speed until smooth and homogeneous.
4. Dice the remaining peaches into 1cm (½in) cubes, add half to the batter and fold them in with a silicone spatula. Pour the batter into the tin then scatter the remaining diced peaches over the top. Bake for 44–46 minutes or until a skewer inserted in the deepest part of the cake comes out clean.
5. Leave the cake in the tin until it is completely cool, then transfer it to a serving plate. Warm the jam for about a minute in the microwave, then brush it over the top of the cake. Pan di pesca keeps for up to 3–4 days under a cake dome.

 nut-free   **PREP TIME:** 20 minutes   **TOTAL BAKING TIME:** 44–46 minutes   **BAKING TEMPERATURE:** 180°C/350°F/Gas mark 4

Berries and ricotta cake

Ricotta is the main ingredient of this cake and, together with Greek yogurt, it produces a dense, sweet and slightly tangy base for the berry compote. Torta frutti rossi e ricotta is particularly easy and fairly quick to make. If made with frozen berries, it can be prepared any time of the year, but it is in the summer, served cold on a sunny afternoon, that this fresh cake gives its best performance. You can, of course, play with the topping and pick the fruit of your choice: apricots, strawberries and peaches work equally well.

SERVES up to 14

for a 27cm (10¾-in) tart tin, preferably loose-based

For the base
butter, for greasing
200g (7oz) egg (about 4 medium eggs), at room temperature
160g (¾ cup plus 1 tbsp) caster (superfine) sugar
⅛ tsp salt
1 tsp vanilla bean paste
350g (1½ cups) ricotta
200g (1 cup) whole Greek-style yogurt (5–10% fat)
zest of 1 unwaxed organic lemon
100g (1 cup) cornflour (cornstarch)

For the topping
350g (12oz) mixed berries (raspberries, blackberries, redcurrants, blackcurrants), fresh or frozen
60g (⅓ cup) caster (superfine) sugar
2 tsp freshly squeezed lemon juice
1 tsp cornflour (cornstarch)
icing (confectioner's) sugar, for dusting

1. Set the shelf in the middle of the oven and preheat it to 180°C/350°F/ Gas mark 4. Grease the tart tin well and line the base with baking paper.
2. Add the eggs, sugar, salt and vanilla to the bowl of a stand mixer with the whisk attachment and whisk at high speed for 6–8 minutes.
3. Meanwhile, add the ricotta to another bowl and cream it using a handheld electric whisk until smooth. Add the yogurt and lemon zest and whisk again to combine.
4. When the eggs look pale and frothy, take the bowl off the stand mixer, sift in the cornflour and fold it in gently with a silicone spatula.
5. Add a couple of ladlefuls of the egg mixture to the creamed ricotta and mix well, then pour this back into the remaining egg mixture and fold until fully combined.
6. Pour the batter into the tart tin and bake for 40–42 minutes, or until the top is a deep caramel colour. Take the cake out of the oven and allow it to cool completely in the tin before turning it onto a serving plate. The centre of the cake will deflate upon cooling, leaving a nice ridge around the edge.
7. Place 250g (9oz) of the berries in a small saucepan, add the sugar and lemon juice and bring to a simmer over a medium heat. Allow the compote to simmer for a couple of minutes, then put 2–3 tablespoonfuls of the juices into a small cup. Add the cornflour to the cup and stir energetically until fully dissolved, then pour the mixture back into the compote. Simmer for another minute then set aside to cool.
8. Once the compote is cooled, fold in the remaining fruit, then spoon it onto the cake and spread evenly. Decorate with a light dusting of icing sugar. Torta frutti rossi e ricotta keeps for up to 3–4 days in the fridge.

PREP TIME: 25 minutes

TOTAL BAKING TIME: 40–42 minutes

BAKING TEMPERATURE: 180°C/350°F/Gas mark 4

gluten-free, nut-free

Upside-down clementine cake

Torta al mandarino is a perfect bake for the winter months, when there is not much fruit available, but clementines are at their best. The flavour is delicate, and I like to give it extra oomph with a touch of natural orange essence. This cake makes an effortless yet eye-catching centrepiece. To avoid doming of the cake, which might make it look awkward when placed upside-down on a serving plate, wrap the tin in a wet cake belt, if you have one. It goes well with a generous dollop of either the yogurt sauce (page 173) or strawberry sauce (page 180).

SERVES up to 12

for a 23cm (9in) springform cake tin

butter, for greasing (use vegetable spread for a dairy-free version)

4 unwaxed organic clementines, plus 2–3 extra fruits for their juice

150g (5½oz) egg (about 3 medium eggs), at room temperature

200g (1 cup) caster (superfine) sugar, plus 2 tbsp for dusting

⅛ tsp salt

1 tsp vanilla bean paste

120g (½ cup plus 1 tbsp) vegetable oil, preferably corn or sunflower

½ tsp natural orange essence (optional)

150g (generous 1 cup) soft wheat 00 flour or plain (all-purpose) flour

80g (generous ⅔ cup) cornflour (cornstarch)

2 tsp baking powder

1. Set the shelf in the lower half of the oven and preheat it to 180°C/ 350°F/Gas mark 4. Grease the tin and line the base with baking paper. Sprinkle 2 tablespoons of sugar on the base of the lined tin.
2. Peel the 4 clementines and very finely chop the peel of 2 fruits (discard the rest). Set aside the peel. Slice the peeled clementines in half horizontally, remove any seeds, and arrange each half, cut-side down, on the sugared baking paper in the base of the tin.
3. Squeeze the extra clementines to make 100g (½ cup) of juice and set aside.
4. Add the eggs, sugar, salt and vanilla to a large bowl and whisk at high speed with a handheld electric whisk (or use a stand mixer) until the sugar has completely dissolved and the mixture is pale and fluffy; it will take about 3–4 minutes. With the whisk still going, trickle the oil into the bowl, add the orange essence (if using) and whisk for about 1 minute to emulsify it fully. Then trickle in the clementine juice and whisk for a further minute.
5. Sift the flour, cornflour and baking powder into the bowl and whisk again at low speed until the batter looks smooth, without any lumps of flour. Add the reserved chopped clementine peel and fold it in with a spatula. Slowly, pour the batter in the tin, making sure that the clementines are not displaced in the process. Wrap the tin in a wet cake belt (if using) and bake for 46–48 minutes, or until a skewer inserted into the deepest part of the cake comes out clean. Leave in the tin to cool for at least 15 minutes.
6. Invert the cake onto a serving plate. Carefully peel off the baking paper to reveal the fruit. Serve at room temperature. Torta al mandarino keeps for up to 3–4 days under a cake dome.

PREP TIME: 20 minutes

TOTAL BAKING TIME: 46–48 minutes

BAKING TEMPERATURE: 180°C/350°F/Gas mark 4

dairy-free, nut-free

TORTA UBRIACA

Drunk chocolate cake

Ubriaco means drunk in Italian, and it is an appropriate name for a cake that uses a decent amount of red wine for the batter and coating. Torta ubriaca has an intense, deep flavour; it is the perfect chocolate cake for grown-ups. The alcohol evaporates entirely while baking, but the cake is left with a complex fragrance that, thanks to the warming spices, is very reminiscent of mulled wine. For extra heat, add a pinch of hot chilli powder, but go carefully, based on the strength of your chillies.

SERVES up to 12

for a 24cm (9½in), 2.5-litre (87-fl oz) bundt tin or a 23cm (9in) springform cake tin

For the sponge
vegetable spread, for greasing
200g (7oz) egg (about 4 medium eggs), at room temperature
230g (1 cup plus 2 tbsp) caster (superfine) sugar
⅛ tsp salt
200g (scant 1 cup) vegetable oil (preferably corn or sunflower)
180g (¾ cup) dry red wine
200g (1½ cups) soft wheat 00 flour or plain (all-purpose) flour, plus extra for dusting
50g (generous ¼ cup) cornflour (cornstarch)
50g (generous ¼ cup) unsweetened cocoa powder
3 tsp baking powder
1 tbsp pisto (see page 21) (alternatively, use 2 tsp ground cinnamon, ½ tsp ground cloves, ¼ tsp ground black pepper and ¼ tsp ground nutmeg)
¼ tsp hot chilli powder (optional)
100g (3½oz) dariy-free dark chocolate chips (50–55% cocoa solids)

For the glaze
120g (¾ cup plus 1 tbsp) icing (confectioner's) sugar
20g (3 tbsp) unsweetened cocoa powder
30g (2 tbsp) red wine
1 tbsp clear honey

1. Set the shelf in the lower half of the oven and preheat it to 160°C/320°C/Gas mark 3. Grease the tin with vegetable spread and dust it with flour, tapping off the excess.
2. Add the eggs, sugar and salt to a bowl large enough to accommodate all the ingredients, and whisk at high speed with a handheld electric whisk (or use a stand mixer) until the sugar has completely dissolved and the mixture is pale and fluffy. It will take about 3–4 minutes. With the whisk still going, trickle the oil into the bowl, and whisk for about 1 minute to emulsify it fully. Then trickle in the wine and whisk for a further minute.
3. Sift the flour, cornflour, cocoa, baking powder, pisto and chilli (if using) into the bowl and whisk again at low speed until the batter looks smooth, without any lumps of flour. Add the chocolate chips and fold them in with a spatula. Pour the batter into the tin and bake for 1 hour 14–16 minutes or until a skewer inserted into the deepest part of the cake comes out clean. Leave in the tin to cool for at least 15 minutes.
4. While the cake cools, put the ingredients for the glaze in a small saucepan and warm over moderate heat until the mixture just starts to simmer.
5. Turn the cake out of the tin and move it to a serving plate. Pour the glaze, while still hot, onto the cake and let it drip over the sides. Serve at room temperature. Torta ubriaca keeps for up to 3–4 days under a cake dome.

PREP TIME: 20 minutes   **TOTAL BAKING TIME:**
1 hour 14–16 minutes   **BAKING TEMPERATURE:**
160°C/320°C/Gas mark 3   dairy-free, nut-free

TORTA ALLE NOCI

Walnut cake

Torta alle noci is another of my family's classics: it uses mostly winter cupboard staples, so it is ideal to brighten up a cold and rainy afternoon. The flavour is unmistakably walnut: nuts are partly ground in the flour mix, partly chopped into larger pieces to add a pleasant crunch. The texture of this cake is pleasantly soft and crumbly: the plump, Marsala-soaked sultanas create an interesting contrast with the crunchy walnuts. The glazing sets to an unusual matte finish; for a shiny look, coat the cake just before serving. It can be served with a caramel (page 181) coffee (page 180) or mascarpone sauce (page 175).

SERVES up to 12

for a 24cm (9½in), 2.5-litre (87-fl oz) bundt tin, or a 23cm springform cake tin

For the sponge
100g (about ¾ cup) sultanas (golden raisins) or raisins
50g (generous 3 tbsp) Marsala or other sweet wine
200g (about 2 cups) walnut pieces
180g (1⅓ cups) soft wheat 00 flour or plain (all-purpose) flour, plus extra for dusting
2 tsp baking powder
100g (scant ½ cup) unsalted butter, plus extra for greasing
200g (7oz) egg (about 4 medium eggs), at room temperature
180g (generous ¾ cup) caster (superfine) sugar
1 tsp vanilla bean paste
⅛ tsp salt
zest of 1 unwaxed organic lemon

For the coating
30g (2 tbsp) clear honey
40g (3 tbsp) Marsala wine
200g (generous 1¼ cups) golden icing (confectioner's) sugar
6 walnut halves, to decorate

1. Set the shelf in the lowest position of the oven and preheat it to 180°C/350°F/Gas mark 4. Grease the tin with butter and dust it with flour, tapping off the excess.

2. Put the sultanas in a small microwave-safe bowl with the Marsala. Heat in the microwave until just warm to the touch: 30 seconds should be enough. Stir, cover with a plate and set aside to soak.

3. Meanwhile, put half the walnuts in the bowl of a food processor, add the flour and baking powder and blitz until the mixture has the texture of fine sand. Set aside. Roughly chop the remaining walnuts with a sharp knife into pea-sized pieces and set aside. Put the butter in a small microwave-safe bowl and melt it: 40 seconds in the microwave should be enough. Set aside to cool. Put the eggs, sugar, vanilla and salt in a bowl large enough to accommodate all the ingredients and whisk at high speed with a handheld electric whisk (or use a stand mixer) for 5 minutes, until the mixture has doubled in volume and is pale and fluffy. Still whisking, slowly trickle in the melted butter then whisk for a further minute to incorporate it fully.

4. Add the walnut and flour mixture to the bowl, add the lemon zest, and fold them in with a silicone spatula. Add the sultanas with the Marsala to the batter, followed by the chopped walnuts, and fold them in gently. Pour the batter into the tin, level the surface with the spatula and bake for 33–35 minutes or until a skewer inserted in the deepest part of the cake comes out clean.

5. Leave the cake in the tin to cool for a few minutes, then turn it onto a wire rack to cool completely. Meanwhile, make the coating. Put the honey and Marsala in a large microwave-safe bowl and microwave for 20 seconds. Add the icing sugar and stir until homogeneous. Set the wire rack over a tray and pour the warm syrup slowly over the top of the cake, coating it completely. Allow the excess to drip off into the tray below. While the coating is still warm, arrange the walnut halves around the cake top. Let the coating set, then transfer the cake to a serving plate. Torta alle noci keeps for up to a week under a cake dome.

PREP TIME: 30 minutes

TOTAL BAKING TIME: 33–35 minutes

BAKING TEMPERATURE: 180°C/350°F/Gas mark 4

Easter cake

Ciambellone di Pasqua is traditionally prepared for Easter in many areas of southern Italy: its fresh and zesty flavour makes it an ideal bake for early spring. Its doughnut shape vaguely recalls the quintessentially Paschal symbol of a nest, and it looks very pretty when decorated with coloured sprinkles over the stark white background of the royal icing.

Despite its attractive looks, the recipe is extremely simple and reasonably robust: it works every single time, making it an ideal bake for less experienced or younger bakers. Even the equipment needed is very sparse: although I recommend the use of an electric whisk, my grandmother used to make this cake literally with one bowl and one fork! For a more grown-up take, swap half the milk for Strega liqueur or, if you want a sweeter flavour, use orange zest and juice instead of lemon. NOTE: The icing for this recipe contains raw egg white and is not suitable for people with weak or compromised immune systems or pregnant women.

SERVES up to 14

for a 24cm (9½in), 2.5-litre (87-fl oz) bundt tin

For the sponge
butter, for greasing
200g (7oz) egg (about 4 medium eggs)
200g (generous 1 cup) caster (superfine) sugar
⅛ tsp salt
1 tsp vanilla bean paste
150g (scant ¾ cup) vegetable oil (preferably sunflower or corn)
100g (½ cup) whole milk
250g (1¾ cups plus 2 tbsp) soft wheat 00 flour or plain (all-purpose) flour, plus extra for dusting
50g (scant ½ cup) cornflour (cornstarch)
2 tsp baking powder
zest and juice of 1 unwaxed organic lemon

For the icing
35g (1¼oz) egg white (about 1 medium egg white)
150g (generous 1 cup) icing (confectioner's) sugar
1 tbsp freshly squeezed lemon juice
coloured sprinkles and small chocolate eggs, to decorate

1. Set the shelf in the lowest position of the oven and preheat it to 180°C/350°F/Gas mark 4. Grease the bundt tin with butter and dust it with flour, tapping off the excess.

2. Add the eggs, sugar, salt and vanilla to a bowl large enough to accommodate all the ingredients and whisk at high speed with a handheld electric whisk (or use a stand mixer) until the sugar has completely dissolved and the mixture is pale and fluffy. It will take about 3–4 minutes. With the whisk still going, slowly trickle the oil then milk into the bowl, and keep whisking for a further minute, until the liquids are fully incorporated.

3. Sift the flour, cornflour and baking powder into the bowl, then add the lemon zest and 2 tablespoons of lemon juice and whisk again until the batter looks smooth, without any lumps of flour. Pour the batter into the tin and bake for 40–45 minutes or until a skewer inserted into the deepest part of the cake comes out clean. Leave in the tin to cool for at least 15 minutes.

4. While the cake cools, whisk the egg white, icing sugar and lemon juice with a handheld electric whisk to stiff peaks, and until the mixture looks stark white.

5. Turn the cake out of the tin and transfer it to a serving plate, top side up. Spoon the icing onto the cake and spread it over the top with the back of the spoon, allowing it to drizzle down the sides. Scatter a couple of tablespoons of sprinkles and decorate with the chocolate eggs. Serve at room temperature once the icing has dried out completely. Ciambellone keeps for up to 3–4 days under a cake dome.

PREP TIME: 20 minutes

TOTAL BAKING TIME: 40–45 minutes

BAKING TEMPERATURE: 180°C/350°F/Gas mark 4

nut-free

MIGLIACCIO
Shrove Tuesday Cake

Migliaccio is named after miglio (millet), the grain that was originally used to make it, nowadays replaced by semolina. It is traditionally baked in Campania on Shrove Tuesday. The recipe is very old, deeply rooted in the local rural culture, and the ingredients are extremely simple: in its basic form, migliaccio is just a baked mix of semolina, ricotta, egg and milk. The result, however, is a truly unmissable and aromatic treat with a creamy yet light texture. The secret is in the accurate balance of the powerful flavourings: after years of tweaking, I have devised this version, where the zesty aroma of the citrus fruit is perfectly balanced by orange blossom, water and cinnamon.

Purists will hate me for this, but I highly recommend adding a handful of dark chocolate chips to the mix; it might not be traditional, but it certainly elevates this cake to a real masterpiece of simplicity.

Migliaccio can be stored in an airtight container or in the fridge, but it should always be wrapped in cling film to avoid drying out. It is best served at room temperature and I suggest dusting with icing sugar just before serving for appeal. To elevate this dessert further, pair it with a dark chocolate (page 177) or coffee sauce (page 180)

SERVES up to 12

for a 23cm/9in springform cake tin

400g (1¾ cups) whole milk
400g (1¾ cups) water
¼ tsp salt
180g (1 cup) semolina
60g (¼ cup) unsalted butter, plus extra for greasing
150g (5½oz) egg (about 3 medium eggs)
250g (1¼ cups) caster (superfine) sugar
250g (generous 1 cup) ricotta, drained
zest of 1 unwaxed organic orange
zest of 1 unwaxed organic lemon
2 tsp vanilla bean paste
½ tsp ground cinnamon
1 tsp orange blossom water
100g (3½oz) dark chocolate chips (50–55% cocoa solids)
icing (confectioner's) sugar, for dusting

1. Set the shelf in the lowest position of the oven and preheat it to 180°C/350°F/Gas mark 4. Grease the tin and line the base with baking paper.
2. Put the milk, water and salt in a medium pan and bring to a simmer over a medium heat. Reduce the heat and gradually add the semolina, sprinkling it in a little at a time, while vigorously and continuously stirring the milk with a whisk to avoid the formation of lumps. Keep stirring for 2–3 minutes to produce a thick paste. Take the pan off the heat and, while it is still hot, add the butter. Stir to melt and incorporate it, then pour the semolina into a wide tray, line the surface with cling film and set aside to cool.
3. Put the eggs and sugar into the bowl of a stand mixer with the whisk attachment. Whisk at high speed until the sugar is fully dissolved and the mixture looks pale and frothy. With the mixer still going, add the drained ricotta, a spoonful at a time, and keep whisking until fully incorporated. Remove the cling film from the fully cooled semolina; it will be rubbery, so break it into large chunks and, while the mixer is still going, add it to the egg mixture in batches, making sure each batch is fully incorporated before adding more. Add the orange and lemon zest, vanilla, cinnamon and orange blossom water to the mixture and whisk to combine. Take the bowl off the mixer, add the chocolate chips and fold them in with a spoon or a spatula.
4. Spoon the batter into the tin and level the surface with the back of the spoon. Bake for 1 hour and 25–30 minutes, or until the edges start browning and the surface turns golden with large cracks; the cake will still have a slight wobble if shaken. Take the cake out of the oven and leave it to cool completely in the tin. It will deflate as soon as it leaves the oven, but this is to be expected. Once cool, transfer the cake to a serving plate. Dust with icing sugar just before serving, using stencils to decorate it. Serve at room temperature and store in an airtight container for up to 3–4 days.

nut-free

PREP TIME: 20 minutes, plus cooling time

TOTAL BAKING TIME: 1 hour 25–30

BAKING TEMPERATURE: 180°C/350°F/Gas mark 4

Pear and prune strudel

Despite looking very different today, strudel and baklava share the same ancestor as well as the same birthplace in the Middle East. From there, predecessors of strudel reached eastern Europe through the extension of the Ottoman Empire, before becoming a staple of Austrian and German cuisine. Today, strudel is officially recognized as a traditional Italian product of the South Tyrol and very much a classic bake in most of north-east Italy.

I have swapped the traditional apple filling for a sweeter pear mixture, combined with juicy prunes, plumped up in cognac: the unmissable spice mix gives it the trademark scent and the addition of flaked almonds provides the necessary crunch. I recommend making the soft dough by hand, because stretching it until it becomes paper-thin is immensely satisfying, but the filling can also be wrapped into shop-bought puff pastry for a quicker result.

You can use any pear variety you have at home, the sweeter the better, as long as the fruits are firm and not watery. Strudel is at its best when served warm with a scoop of vanilla ice cream or a drizzle of double cream.

SERVES up to 14

For the pastry
150g (1 cup plus 2 tbsp) soft wheat 00 flour or plain (all-purpose) flour, plus extra for dusting
30g (2 tbsp) water
50g (1¾oz) egg (about 1 medium egg), at room temperature
20g (1½ tbsp) unsalted butter, at room temperature and diced
10g (2 tsp) caster (superfine) sugar
⅛ tsp salt

For the filling
100g (about ¾ cup) dried pitted prunes
70g (5 tbsp) cognac or brandy
400g (14oz) Conference or Williams pears (2 medium or 3 smaller fruits)
80g (scant ½ cup) dark soft brown sugar
40g (about ½ cup) flaked almonds
zest and juice of 1 unwaxed organic lemon
½ tsp ground cinnamon
½ tsp ground ginger
¼ tsp ground cloves

1. Chop the prunes into 1cm (½in) pieces, put in a bowl large enough to accommodate all the filling ingredients and add the cognac. Cover with a plate and leave to soak.

2. Put the flour, water, egg, butter, caster sugar and salt in a medium bowl. Mix with a spoon first, then by hand until the mixture comes together in a dough. Turn it out onto a clean and dry worktop and knead it for about 10 minutes, or until the dough becomes smooth and elastic, and does not break easily when pinched and stretched. Leave the dough on the worktop, cover it with the bowl and let it rest for at least 20 minutes.

3. Peel, core and dice the pears into pea-sized pieces, then add them to the bowl with the prunes, brown sugar, almonds, lemon zest, cinnamon, ginger and cloves. Squeeze the zested lemon and add 1 tablespoon of juice to the same bowl; mix thoroughly to combine and set aside.

4. Set the shelf in the lower half of the oven and preheat it to 180°C/350°F/ Gas mark 4. Place the butter in a small microwave-safe bowl and melt it: 25–30 seconds in the microwave should be enough. Set aside to cool.

5. Roll out the pastry on a lightly floured worktop to a thickness of 2mm (1⁄16in). Transfer it to a large sheet of baking paper then stretch it gently by hand to shape it as a 40 x 50cm (16 x 20in) rectangle. Brush generously with the melted butter.

6. Turn the pastry so that its shorter side faces you. Scatter half the breadcrumbs over the bottom two-thirds of the dough. Add the remaining breadcrumbs to the fruit mixture and stir to incorporate them. Spoon the filling over the pastry, distributing it evenly over the bottom two-thirds of the dough only.

Recipe continues overleaf

PREP TIME: 40 minutes, plus resting time

TOTAL BAKING TIME: 40-45 minutes

BAKING TEMPERATURE: 180°C/350°F/Gas mark 4

For the assembly
40g (3 tbsp) unsalted
    butter, for brushing
40g (scant ½ cup)
    dried breadcrumbs
1 egg yolk
1 tbsp whole milk
1 tbsp dark soft
    brown sugar
icing (confectioner's)
    sugar, for dusting

7. Roll up the strudel starting from the side closest to you and using the baking paper to help lift the dough. Once the strudel is shaped, roll it on the baking paper so that the join is underneath, then pinch the sides to seal them. Slide the strudel and the baking paper onto a baking sheet. Beat the egg yolk with the milk to make an egg wash and brush the top of the strudel with it. Sprinkle it with the brown sugar, then cut several diagonal slits on top with a sharp knife, about 2cm (1in) apart. Bake for 40–45 minutes or until the pastry has browned all over. When ready to serve, dust lightly with icing sugar. Strudel pere e prugne is best served within a day of baking and ideally while it is still warm.

CHEESECAKE CAFFÈ E AMARETTI

Amaretti and coffee cheesecake

Although cheesecakes do not belong to the classic Italian baking register, they are so popular that they have found their way into pretty much every family recipe book. An ideal cake for beginners, this recipe requires no baking and combines two of my favourite flavours; coffee liqueur and amaretti provide a pleasantly bitter flavour, so the overall result is not overly sweet. For a non-alcoholic version, you can swap the Kahlúa for strong coffee.

Mascarpone gives the cream an unbeatable velvety texture, and the ricotta keeps it lighter and surprisingly smooth. I like to fold whipped cream into my cheesecake as this opens up the otherwise dense structure. Despite its rather simple looks, this cake is bound to trigger many thumbs-up around the table and leave your guests asking for more.

SERVES up to 12

for a 23cm (9in) springform cake tin

For the base
90g (scant ½ cup) unsalted butter
200g (7oz) amaretti biscuits
⅛ tsp salt

For the cream
4 platinum-grade gelatine sheets (about 8g/⅙oz) or 16g (½oz) standard powdered gelatine
4 tsp instant coffee granules
100g (scant ½ cup) hot water
250g (generous 1 cup) mascarpone, at room temperature
120g (½ cup) ricotta, drained and at room temperature
100g (generous ¾ cup) icing (confectioner's) sugar
1 tsp vanilla bean paste
40g (about 3 tbsp) Kahlúa coffee liqueur
200g (¾ cup plus 1 tbsp) whipping (heavy) cream (35–40% fat), cold
12 amaretti, to decorate

1. Line the base of the tin with baking paper. Place the gelatine sheets in a small bowl and cover them with cold water; leave to soak for about 10 minutes.
2. Put the butter in a small microwave-safe bowl and melt it in the microwave: 30–40 seconds should be enough. Set aside to cool.
3. Put the amaretti and salt in the bowl of a food processor and blitz until they resemble sand. Transfer to a medium bowl and add the melted butter. Mix to moisten the crushed amaretti fully, then tip the mixture into the lined tin. Press it down firmly using the back of a spoon or the bottom of a cup. Put in the fridge to set.
4. Dissolve the coffee in the hot water, drain the soaked gelatine and dissolve the sheets in the hot coffee by whisking energetically for a few seconds. Set aside to cool.
5. Put the mascarpone, ricotta, sugar and vanilla in a bowl large enough to accommodate all the ingredients, then whisk by hand or with a handheld electric whisk until smooth and homogeneous. Add the cooled coffee mixture and the coffee liqueur and whisk again until well combined.
6. Put the whipping cream in another bowl and whisk until it forms soft peaks. Do not overbeat or it will curdle: stop as soon as the surface changes from shiny to dull. Use a silicone spatula to gently fold the cream into the mascarpone-coffee mixture in three batches.
7. Pour or spoon the mixture over the biscuit base, level it off with the back of a spoon or, better, with a small offset spatula, then chill in the fridge for at least 5 hours or overnight.
8. When ready to serve, loosen the sides of the cheesecake with a small knife, remove the ring of the tin and transfer the cake to a serving plate. Decorate the top with amaretti. Cheesecake caffè e amaretti keeps for up to 3 days in the fridge.

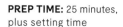

PREP TIME: 25 minutes, plus setting time

SETTING TIME: 5 hours

Date cake

Originally from North Africa, torta di datteri crossed the Mediterranean and gained popularity in Italy. It is a flavoursome cake, with a substantial bite and a dense yet soft crumb. The recipe does not include any leavening agent, so the egg whites have to be whipped separately and gently folded into the batter to incorporate as much air as possible. The crunch of walnuts and almonds is a good match for the sticky and chewy texture of the dates, and the added nutty flavour is perfectly paired with the citrus undertones. It goes particularly well with a strong cup of tea or flowery herbal infusion, like hibiscus. NOTE: The icing for this recipe contains raw egg white and is not suitable for people with weak or compromised immune systems or pregnant women.

SERVES up to 12

for a 24cm (9½in), 2.5-litre (87fl oz) bundt tin or a 23cm (9in) springform cake tin

For the sponge
80g (⅓ cup) unsalted butter, plus extra for greasing
100g (about 1 cup) walnut pieces
100g (about ¾ cup) whole almonds
40g (scant ⅓ cup) cornflour (cornstarch)
250g (9oz) whole dates
1 tbsp clear honey
zest of 1 unwaxed organic lemon
zest of 1 unwaxed organic orange
40g (8 tsp) freshly squeezed orange juice
60g (2¼oz) egg yolk and 140g (5oz) egg white (about 4 medium eggs), at room temperature
80g (about ⅔ cup) golden icing (confectioner's) sugar
1 tsp vanilla bean paste
⅛ tsp salt

For the decoration
35g (1¼oz) egg white (about 1 medium egg white)
200g (generous 1¾ cups) icing (confectioner's) sugar
2–3 tbsp freshly squeezed lemon juice (about 1 lemon)
2–3 dates, pitted and sliced lengthways into slivers

1. Set the shelf in the lower half of the oven and preheat it to 200°C/400°F/Gas mark 6. Grease the tin with butter and dust it with flour, tapping out the excess. Put the butter in a small microwave-safe bowl and melt it: 30–40 seconds in the microwave should be enough. Set aside to cool.

2. Put the walnuts, almonds and cornflour in the bowl of a food processor and blitz to a coarse texture. Set aside. Stone and chop the dates into pea-sized pieces, then put in a medium bowl with the honey, lemon and orange zest, orange juice and melted butter. Stir well to combine.

3. Put the egg yolks, half the icing sugar and the vanilla in another bowl, large enough to accommodate all the ingredients, and whisk at high speed with a handheld electric whisk (or use a stand mixer) until the mixture is pale and fluffy. It will take about 3–4 minutes. Add the date mixture and the ground nuts to the bowl and fold in. Set aside.

4. Thoroughly wash and dry the whisk. Put the egg whites and salt in a clean bowl, preferably metal, ceramic or glass, and whisk at medium speed for about a minute or until the whisk leaves visible marks on the egg-white surface. Continue whisking and gradually add the remaining icing sugar to form a stiff but supple meringue; it will take about 2 minutes.

5. Spoon the meringue into the nut and date mixture in three goes, folding it in gently after each addition until no more white streaks are visible. Spoon or pour the batter into the greased tin and bake for 33–35 minutes, until well browned and springy. Leave to cool in the tin for a few minutes, then turn it out on a wire rack to cool completely.

6. Once the cake has cooled, whisk the egg white, icing sugar and 1 tablespoon of the lemon juice for about 3–4 minutes until the mixture is fluffy but still supple. Gradually stir in by hand 1–2 tablespoons of the remaining lemon juice until the icing is of a thick dropping consistency. Spoon or pour it sparingly over the top of the cake, letting some to drip down the sides. You may not need all of the icing. Decorate the top with thin slivers of date. Torta di datteri keeps for up to 3–4 days under a cake dome.

PREP TIME: 35 minutes | **TOTAL BAKING TIME:** 33–35 minutes | **BAKING TEMPERATURE:** 200°C/400°F/Gas mark 6 | gluten-free

TORTA COCCO E AMARENA

Coconut and Amarena cherry cake

If you try one cake from this book, it has to be torta cocco e Amarena. Not a traditional Italian bake per se, this cake is the result of... a baker's epiphany. My obsession with Amarena cherries is borderline pathological: I never miss an opportunity to add a spoonful to my desserts. I have a soft spot for coconut too: the scent and flavour of the exotic fruit bring back memories of days spent lounging in the scorching sun of Italian summers. Only a few years ago, it occurred to me that I could bring my two beloved flavours together in a single bake, and this cake was born. It is everything you want a good cake to be: light but with a satisfying bite, aromatic, bursting with flavour, and with a perfect balance of sweetness and tanginess. Amarena cherries in syrup are widely available in specialist shops or through online retailers (page 19). It takes less than 20 minutes to prepare this cake but I guarantee that, once baked, it will last even less time!

SERVES up to 12

for a 24cm (9½in), 2.5 litre (87fl oz) bundt tin, or a 23cm (9in) springform cake tin

butter, for greasing
100g (3½oz) egg (about 2 medium eggs), at room temperature
120g (⅔ cup) caster (superfine) sugar
1 tsp vanilla bean paste
50g (scant ¼ cup) vegetable oil (preferably corn or sunflower)
150g (scant ¾ cup) whole natural yogurt
100g (¾ cup) soft wheat 00 flour or plain (all-purpose) flour, plus extra for dusting
2 tsp baking powder
70g (about 1 cup) unsweetened desiccated (shredded) coconut
200g (7oz) Amarena cherries in syrup, drained

1. Set the shelf in the lowest position of the oven and preheat it to 180°C/350°F/Gas mark 4. Grease the tin with butter and dust it with flour, tapping off the excess.
2. Put the eggs, sugar and vanilla in a bowl large enough to accommodate all the ingredients and whisk with a handheld electric whisk (or use a stand mixer) at high speed until the sugar has completely dissolved and the mixture is pale and fluffy; it will take about 3–4 minutes. Still whisking, slowly trickle first the oil and then the yogurt into the bowl. Keep whisking for another minute until the liquids are fully incorporated.
3. Sift the flour and baking powder into the bowl, add the coconut and mix at low speed until well blended. Pour the batter into the tin, then scatter the drained cherries evenly across the top of the batter; they will sink into the batter while baking. Bake for 34–35 minutes or until the top is a rich caramel colour and a skewer inserted in the deepest part of the cake comes out clean.
4. Leave the cake to cool in the tin for at least 15 minutes, then turn it out onto a wire rack to cool completely. Serve at room temperature. Torta cocco e Amarena keeps for up to 3 days under a cake dome.

● nut-free

PREP TIME: 20 minutes

TOTAL BAKING TIME: 34–35 minutes

BAKING TEMPERATURE: 180°C/350°F/Gas mark 4

PREP TIME: 45 minutes, plus cooling time

TOTAL BAKING TIME: 46–48 minutes

BAKING TEMPERATURE: 180°C/350°F/Gas mark 4

Cherry crumble tart

Sbriciolata, not to be confused with sbrisolona (page 157), is a modern interpretation of the classic crostata. It delivers all the buttery crumbliness of a conventional tart without any pastry rolling, cutting or decorating. The pastry is not made into the usual doughy mass, but it is left in a crumbly state, so the flakes (briciole in Italian) can be simply scattered into the tin.

The look is rustic, but the cleverly crafted rough-and-ready top makes it elegant and appealing, albeit deceptively simple. The pastry takes no longer than 5 minutes to prepare, which makes it very popular among home bakers: versions are proposed with a wide variety of fillings, to suit every taste. My recipe includes a cherry and apple compote, with just the right balance of sweet and sour. However, the tart can be filled with shop-bought jam if you prefer or even, when you are feeling particularly decadent, with a jar of chocolate spread.

SERVES up to 14

for a 27cm (10¾in) tart tin, preferably loose-based

For the pastry

420g (scant 3¼ cups) soft wheat 00 flour or plain (all-purpose) flour, plus extra for dusting
¾ tsp baking powder
50g (½ cup) ground almonds
210g (generous 1 cup) caster (superfine) sugar
1 tsp vanilla bean paste
zest of 1 unwaxed organic lemon
¼ tsp salt
100g (3½oz) egg (about 2 medium eggs), cold
170g (¾ cup) unsalted butter, cold and diced, plus extra for greasing
icing (confectioner's) sugar, for dusting

For the filling

100g (½ cup) caster (superfine) sugar
15g (2 tbsp) cornflour (cornstarch)
300g (10½oz) sweet apples (about 2 medium fruits)
400g (14oz) frozen pitted cherries
2 tbsp freshly squeezed lemon juice

1. Grease the tin with butter and dust it with flour, tapping off the excess. Line the base with baking paper.
2. Sift the flour and baking powder into the bowl of a stand mixer with the paddle attachment. Add the ground almonds, sugar, vanilla, lemon zest and salt, then mix with a spoon until fully combined. Whisk the eggs and add them to the bowl with the butter, then mix on the lowest speed for a few seconds – just enough for the ingredients to form a rough, flaky crumble. Stop the mixer as soon as possible or you will end up with a conventional pastry dough.
3. Spoon just over half of the mixture (600g/1lb 5oz) into the lined tin and gently press it down with your fingertips or with the base of a cup, roughly lining the sides of the tin as well. Chill both the lined tin and the remaining mixture in the fridge.
4. For the filling, put the sugar and cornflour in a medium saucepan and stir them well until the cornflour is fully dispersed into the sugar. Peel and core the apples, dice them in pea-sized pieces and add them to the pan, together with the cherries and lemon juice. Cook, covered with a lid, over a low heat for about 15 minutes, stirring occasionally, until all the juices are running and the cherries have defrosted. Increase the heat to medium, remove the lid and bring to a simmer. Cook, stirring regularly for a further 6–7 minutes, or until the juices are thick and syrupy. Leave to cool for a few minutes then transfer to the fridge to cool completely.
5. When ready to bake, set the shelf in the lower half of the oven and preheat it to 180°C/350°F/Gas mark 4.
6. Spoon the filling into the pastry-lined tin, levelling it out with the back of a spoon. Scatter the remaining crumble mixture over the filling without compacting it. The mixture will cover most, but not all the filling. Bake for 46–48 minutes or until the edges of the tart start to turn golden brown.
7. Let the tart cool completely in the tin before demoulding, then transfer it to a serving dish and decorate it with a light dusting of icing sugar. Sbriciolata alle ciliegie keeps for up to 3 days under a cake dome.

CUOR DI SICILIA

Sunken ricotta cake

Few things epitomize the simplicity of Italian baking like the filling of Sicilian cannoli: a straightforward mix of cheap ingredients – ricotta, sugar and candied orange peel – delivers the freshest and most flavoursome cream, ready literally in a matter of seconds.

Admittedly, making cannoli shells is rather time consuming, so I translated the addictive flavour and texture of their filling into cake form. Cuor di Sicilia is named after the land that created cannoli and it is ready to bake in less than half an hour: the ricotta cream is piped as a substantial noodle across the surface of the batter so that it gently sinks into the cake as it bakes, leaving a pretty zig-zag trail behind. Despite its simplicity, this cake is bound to surprise your guests: each slice has a core of the delicious filling surrounded by a soft marsala- and orange-flavoured sponge.

SERVES up to 14

for a 30 x 12cm (12 x 4½in), 1.5-litre (52fl oz) loaf tin

For the cream
250g (generous 1 cup) ricotta, drained
40g (scant ¼ cup) caster (superfine) sugar
1 tsp vanilla bean paste
zest of 1 unwaxed organic orange
20g (1 tbsp) mixed candied peel (page 150), finely diced (no bigger than 5mm/¼in)
20g (1 tbsp) dark chocolate drops (70–75% cocoa solids)

For the sponge
150g (5½oz) egg (about 3 medium eggs)
150g (¾ cup) caster (superfine) sugar
1 tsp vanilla bean paste
90g (¼ cup plus 3 tbsp) vegetable oil (preferably corn or sunflower)
60g (4 tbsp) Marsala wine
220g (1⅔ cups) soft wheat 00 flour or plain (all-purpose) flour
2 tsp baking powder
zest of 1 unwaxed organic orange
icing (confectioner's) sugar for dusting

1. Set the shelf in the lowest position of the oven and preheat it to 180°C/350°F/Gas mark 4. Grease the tin and line it with baking paper.
2. Put the ricotta in a bowl large enough to accommodate all the ingredients for the cream. Stir with a balloon whisk until smooth, then add the sugar, vanilla and orange zest and whisk to combine. Add the candied peel and chocolate drops and mix to incorporate. Transfer the cream to a disposable piping bag without a nozzle, twist or clip the top closed and chill in the fridge until needed.
3. Add the eggs, sugar and vanilla to a bowl large enough to accommodate all the sponge ingredients. Whisk with a handheld electric whisk (or use a stand mixer) at high speed, until the sugar has completely dissolved and the mixture is pale and fluffy; it will take about 4–5 minutes. Still whisking, slowly trickle first the oil then the Marsala into the bowl and keep whisking for another minute until the liquids are fully incorporated.
4. Sift the flour and baking powder into the bowl, then add the orange zest and fold them in by hand with a silicone spatula, until the batter looks smooth, without any lumps of flour. Pour the batter into the lined tin and level it out with the back of a spoon or spatula. Snip the end of the piping bag with the ricotta mixture to 2cm (1in) width and pipe the cream over the top of the batter in a zig-zag pattern. The ricotta cream must sit on the batter and not be stirred in; it will sink into the batter while baking.
5. Bake for 48–50 minutes or until a skewer inserted into the sponge comes out clean. Make sure you avoid inserting the skewer into the cream or the moisture from the ricotta will give you a false reading. Leave the cake in the tin to cool for at least 10 minutes before turning it out onto a wire rack to cool completely. When ready to serve, transfer the cake to a serving plate and decorate the top with a light dusting of icing sugar. Cuor di Sicilia keeps for up to 3 days under a cake dome.

● nut-free

PREP TIME:
25 minutes

TOTAL BAKING TIME:
48–50 minutes

BAKING TEMPERATURE:
180°C/350°F/Gas mark 4

CAKELETS

Camille	60
Tortine all'arancia	62
Tortine ai fichi	64
Tortine barbabietola e cioccolato	66
Tortine cioccolato e pere	68
Tortine castagne e cioccolato	70
Plumcakes	72
Gobeletti	74
Crostatine al marzapane	76
Cuore morbido al gianduja	78
Tortine alla polenta	80
Parrozzini	82
Tartellette alla frutta	85
Fetta al latte	88

CAMILLE

Carrot cupcakes

Camille are the Italian counterpart of the classic carrot cake: this Mediterranean version rounds off the sweetness of the carrots with the tanginess of oranges and a hint of almonds. The result is a soft cakelet with a not-overly sweet flavour and a zesty aftertaste. This recipe can also be baked in a conventional tin and morphed into an unusual carrot cake; however, I prefer to make a batch of cakelets, topped with toasted almonds and a glistening coating of orange marmalade.

Traditionally served for breakfast, camille are a welcome treat any time of the day, perfect for elevenses and ideal as an afternoon snack for kids and grown-ups alike.

MAKES 12

220g (8oz) carrots, peeled and roughly chopped
100g (3½oz) egg (about 2 medium eggs), at room temperature
180g (generous ¾ cup) light brown soft sugar
1 tsp vanilla bean paste
¼ tsp salt
100g (scant ½ cup) vegetable oil (preferably sunflower or corn)
zest of 1 unwaxed organic orange
270g (2 cups) soft wheat 00 flour or plain (all-purpose) flour
3 tsp baking powder
2 tsp ground cinnamon
1 tsp ground ginger
110g (about 1 cup) ground almonds
130g (½ cup) freshly squeezed orange juice (about 2 medium oranges)
50g (about ½ cup) toasted flaked almonds
100g (3½oz) orange marmalade

1. Set the shelf in the middle of the oven and preheat it to 180°C/350°F/Gas mark 4. Line a 12-hole muffin tray with paper cases.
2. Put the chopped carrots in the bowl of a food processor and blitz them finely. Put the eggs, sugar, vanilla and salt in the bowl of a stand mixer with the whisk attachment and whisk at high speed until the mixture is pale and frothy; it will take about 5 minutes. Still whisking, slowly trickle the oil into the bowl and continue to whisk for a further minute to incorporate it fully.
3. Swap the whisk for the paddle attachment, then add the orange zest and carrots to the bowl and mix at the lowest speed until the carrots are just incorporated into the batter.
4. Sift the flour, baking powder, cinnamon and ginger into the bowl and mix again at minimum speed until homogeneous. Add the ground almonds and, with the mixer running at low speed, trickle in the orange juice. Once the batter is homogeneous, distribute it into the paper cases with a spoon (or an ice-cream scoop), filling them to 1cm (½in) from the rim.
5. Scatter a generous pinch of flaked almonds on each cakelet and bake for 24–25 minutes, or until the tops are a deep golden colour and a skewer inserted into the centre comes out clean. Remove from the oven and let them cool slightly.
6. Meanwhile, warm the marmalade for about 1 minute in the microwave, then brush it over the tops of the cakes and leave to cool completely. Camille keep for up to 3 days under a cake dome.

dairy-free   **PREP TIME:** 25 minutes   **TOTAL BAKING TIME:** 24–25 minutes   **BAKING TEMPERATURE:** 180°C/350°F/Gas mark 4

Orange cupcakes

Tortine all'arancia are inspired by pan d'arancio, an orange-flavoured cake originally from Sicily. They are arguably the easiest and quickest treat I have ever learnt to bake. It takes less than 15 minutes to prepare the batter, which is made entirely in a food processor: there is nothing to whip or pipe so you will be left with very little washing-up too.

The recipe is another one that is ideal for younger or less experienced bakers to tackle, but do not be fooled: despite being super-simple to make, these cupcakes are extraordinarily flavoursome. The high orange juice content gives the crumb unparalleled softness, and the peel gives it a kick that is both moreish and sophisticated. Your kitchen will smell amazing while baking these little treats! Tortine all'arancia can be prepared in advance and even frozen, so they are ideal for picnics or an afternoon with friends.

MAKES 12

320g (11oz) unwaxed organic oranges (about 2 medium oranges)
120g (4¼oz) egg (about 2 large eggs)
80g (¼ cup plus 2 tbsp) vegetable oil (preferably corn or sunflower)
80g (¼ cup plus 2 tbsp) whole milk
1 tsp vanilla bean paste
250g (1¾ cups plus 2 tbsp) soft wheat 00 flour or plain (all-purpose) flour
2 tsp baking powder
250g (1½ cups) caster (superfine) sugar
⅛ tsp salt
1 unwaxed organic orange, to decorate
50g (generous ⅓ cup) icing (confectioner's) sugar

1. Set the shelf in the middle of the oven and preheat it to 180°C/350°F/ Gas mark 4. Line a 12-hole muffin tray with muffin cases.
2. Wash and dry the oranges, then slice off the top and bottom ends. Dice the rest roughly, place them in the bowl of a food processor and blitz to a pulp. Add the eggs, oil, milk and vanilla to the same bowl and blitz again at high speed for about 1 minute, or until the mixture is smooth. Add the flour, baking powder, sugar and salt and give it a short final blitz just to incorporate the dry ingredients. Scrape down the sides of the bowl with a silicone spatula, if necessary.
3. Spoon or pour the batter in the muffin cases, filling them to two-thirds full (an ice-cream scoop is ideal for this), then bake for 25–27 minutes or until the tops are a deep golden colour and a skewer inserted into the centre comes out clean.
4. Take the cupcakes out of the oven and leave them to cool slightly. Meanwhile, zest the orange with a vegetable peeler and slice the zest into thin strips. Squeeze the zested orange and mix 2 teaspoons of its juice with the icing sugar to make a simple glaze; if too thick, add a third teaspoon of juice. Drizzle the glaze over the cupcakes with a spoon and scatter the strips of zest over the cupcakes before the glaze sets. The cupcakes keep for 3–4 days under a cake dome, or they can be frozen for up to a month.

TORTINE AI FICHI
<u>Sticky fig cupcakes</u>

Figs grow wild and in abundance pretty much everywhere in southern Italy and, when perfectly ripe, they are as sweet and delicious as the most exotic and expensive pastry. Including a generous helping of these glistening jewels in a simple cupcake has been nothing short of a revelation: I have been baking these cupcakes for years and I have yet to find someone who is not completely taken by their delicate flavour and indulgent texture.

The orangey aftertaste matches perfectly with the figs' sweetness and the honey-based syrup replicates the typical stickiness of these fruits. Perhaps tortine ai fichi should be served with an etiquette warning: it will be extremely difficult to resist the temptation to lick your fingers!

MAKES 12

200g (7oz) fresh figs (about 5 medium fruits)
120g (½ cup) unsalted butter, softened
200g (generous 1 cup) caster (superfine) sugar
¼ tsp salt
120g (4¼oz) egg (about 2 large eggs), at room temperature
1 tsp vanilla bean paste
zest and juice of 1 unwaxed organic orange
250g (1¾ cups plus 2 tbsp) soft wheat 00 flour or plain (all-purpose) flour
2 tsp baking powder
½ tsp ground cinnamon
120g (½ cup) whole milk
40g (8 tsp) clear honey

1. Wash and pat the figs dry, remove their stalks and dice the fruits into pea-sized pieces. Set the shelf in the middle of the oven and preheat it to 180°C/350°F/Gas mark 4. Line a 12-hole muffin tray with muffin cases.
2. Put the butter into the bowl of a stand mixer with the paddle attachment, add the sugar and salt, and cream the mixture at high speed until light and fluffy. Add the eggs, vanilla and orange zest, and keep beating until fully incorporated, scraping down the sides of the bowl as needed. Sift in the flour, baking powder and cinnamon, then mix again at the lowest setting, just long enough to incorporate the dry ingredients. Add the milk and mix one final time to incorporate it. Take the bowl off the stand mixer, add two-thirds of the diced figs and fold them in with a silicone spatula. Spoon the batter into the muffin cases, filling them to two-thirds full (an ice-cream scoop is ideal for this). Scatter the remaining figs over the surface of the cupcakes then bake for 25–27 minutes until the tops are golden and a skewer inserted into the centre comes out clean.
3. Meanwhile, pour the orange juice into a small saucepan and add the honey. Place over a moderate heat and stir until the honey is fully dissolved and the syrup just starts to simmer. As soon as the cupcakes are out of the oven, brush their tops with the hot syrup, using a pastry brush. Leave the cupcakes to cool completely in the tray, then transfer them to a serving plate. Tortine ai fichi keep for up to 3 days under a cake dome.

 nut-free   **PREP TIME:** 20 minutes   **TOTAL BAKING TIME:** 25–27 minutes   **BAKING TEMPERATURE:** 180°C/350°F/Gas mark 4

TORTINE BARBABIETOLA E CIOCCOLATO

Beetroot and chocolate cupcakes

The first time I heard of beetroot in a cake, I scoffed. But after testing the beetroot and chocolate combination, I went back several times, and now these cupcakes have become a family favourite. The earthy sweetness of beetroots adds richness to the chocolate and the moisture they bring to the batter delivers an exceptionally soft sponge. The mascarpone frosting is the perfect complement to the chocolatey cake: light but indulgent and with a gentle hint of orange. I always use ready-to-eat, unseasoned beetroots, the type sold vacuum-packed, but you can certainly cook them from fresh.

MAKES 12

For the sponge
200g (7oz) cooked
  beetroot (beets)
80g (2¾oz) dark chocolate
  chips, or bar broken into
  small pieces (70–75%
  cocoa solids)
100g (3½oz) egg (about 2
  medium eggs), at room
  temperature
120g (⅔ cup) caster
  (superfine) sugar
⅛ tsp salt
130g (½ cup plus 2 tbsp)
  vegetable oil (preferably
  corn or sunflower)
160g (scant 1¼ cups) soft
  wheat 00 flour or plain
  (all-purpose) flour
1½ tsp baking powder
zest of 1 unwaxed organic
  orange
12 chocolate buttons,
  to decorate

For the frosting
170g (½ cup plus 3 tbsp)
  mascarpone
80g (about ⅔ cup) icing
  (confectioner's) sugar
½ tsp natural orange
  essence
160g (½ cup plus 2 tbsp)
  whipping (heavy) cream
  (35–40% fat)

1. Set the shelf in the middle of the oven and preheat it to 180°C/350°F/Gas mark 4. Line a 12-hole muffin tray with muffin cases.

2. Roughly chop the beetroots and blitz them in a food processor to make a fine purée. Set aside.

3. Put the chocolate in a small bowl and microwave it for 30 seconds, then stir well and keep microwaving it in 5-second bursts, stirring well between subsequent bursts until completely melted. Set aside to cool.

4. Put the eggs, sugar and salt in a large bowl and whisk with a handheld electric whisk (or use a stand mixer) at high speed, until the sugar has dissolved and the mixture is pale and fluffy, for about 5 minutes. Still whisking, slowly trickle the oil into the bowl, followed by the melted chocolate and the beetroot purée, and keep whisking for a further minute, until the liquids are fully incorporated.

5. Sift the flour and baking powder into the bowl, then add the orange zest and whisk again at medium speed until the batter is smooth, without any lumps of flour. Scrape down the sides of the bowl with a silicone spatula, if necessary.

6. Spoon or pour the batter into the muffin cases, filling them to 5mm (¼in) from the rim. Bake immediately for 21–23 minutes, or until a skewer inserted into the deepest part of one comes out clean. Let the cupcakes cool in the tray for 5 minutes, then transfer to a wire rack to cool completely.

7. Meanwhile, in a bowl, beat the mascarpone, icing sugar and orange essence with a handheld electric whisk at medium speed, just long enough to combine the ingredients. Add the cream and increase the speed. Whisk the mixture until it forms soft peaks that hold their shape. Do not overdo it or it will curdle: stop once the surface changes from shiny to dull. Store the frosting in the fridge until ready to use.

8. Once the cupcakes have cooled completely, top them with a generous helping of frosting: you can spoon it, spread it or pipe it. I like to use an 18mm (¾in) star nozzle, but all methods will work well. Decorate the top of each cupcake with a chocolate button. Tortine barbabietola e cioccolato must be stored in the fridge and used within 3 days.

---

 nut-free   **PREP TIME:** 35 minutes   **TOTAL BAKING TIME:**
21-23 minutes   **BAKING TEMPERATURE:**
180°C/350°F/Gas mark 4

Chocolate and pear cupcakes

The pear and dark chocolate combination is a classic of modern Italian patisserie, and for very good reasons. If you ever have the chance to visit an Italian ice-cream parlour, ask for a scoop of each flavour and you too will fall in love with it.

The delicate sweetness of the pears blends with and balances out the dominant flavour of the chocolate to deliver a fruity, flavoursome and chocolatey cake. The extra pear in the batter keeps it fresh and moist, creating a unique and irresistible texture.

I typically use Williams or Conference pears; however, you can use whatever variety you have, as long as the fruits are not too ripe or watery.

MAKES 12

360g (12oz) pears (about 2 medium fruits)
120g (4¼oz) egg (about 2 large eggs), at room temperature
130g (⅔ cup) caster (superfine) sugar
1 tsp vanilla bean paste
⅛ tsp salt
50g (scant ¼ cup) vegetable oil
70g (scant ⅓ cup) whole milk
130g (1 cup) soft wheat 00 flour or plain (all-purpose) flour
1½ tsp baking powder
30g (4 tbsp) unsweetened cocoa powder
½ tsp ground ginger

1. Wash and pat the pears dry. Chop one fruit into pea-sized pieces, discarding the core. Quarter the other pear, discarding the top and the core, and slice it into thin wedges. Set aside for later. Set the shelf in the middle of the oven and preheat it to 180°C/350°F/Gas mark 4. Line a 12-hole muffin tray with muffin cases.
2. Put the eggs, sugar, vanilla and salt in a bowl large enough to accommodate all the ingredients and whisk with a handheld electric whisk (or use a stand mixer) at high speed, until the sugar has completely dissolved and the mixture is pale and fluffy. It will take about 4–5 minutes. Still whisking, slowly trickle first the oil and then the milk into the bowl and keep whisking for a further minute until the liquids are fully incorporated.
3. Sift the flour, baking powder, cocoa powder and ginger into the bowl, then mix at low speed until the batter is smooth and homogeneous, without any lumps of flour. Add the diced pears to the batter and fold them in by hand.
4. Spoon the batter into the muffin cases, filling them up to three-quarters – an ice-cream scoop is ideal for this job. Carefully arrange the pear slices over the surface of the cupcakes then bake for 24–25 minutes until a skewer inserted into the deepest part of one comes out clean. Let the cupcakes cool in the tray for 5 minutes, then transfer them to a wire rack to cool completely. Tortine cioccolato e pere keep for up to 3 days under a cake dome.

PREP TIME: 25 minutes | **TOTAL BAKING TIME:** 24-25 minutes | **BAKING TEMPERATURE:** 180°C/350°F/Gas mark 4 | nut-free

TORTINE CASTAGNE E CIOCCOLATO

Chestnut and chocolate cakelets

The comforting flavour of tortine castagne e cioccolato makes them ideal to warm the first chilly autumnal nights. Chestnut flour not only makes them naturally gluten-free, it also adds a hint of nuttiness to the chocolate flavour and provides a unique, melt-in-the-mouth, almost creamy quality to the texture.

I recommend serving these cakelets accompanied by lashings of sweet whipped cream or, even better, by a generous glug of raspberry sauce (page 180). I bake them in mini-cake moulds, but they can also be baked as cupcakes in a conventional muffin tray.

MAKES 12 cupcakes or 24 mini-cakes

100g (3½oz) dark chocolate chips, or bar broken into small pieces (50–55% cocoa solids)
50g (3½ tbsp) unsalted butter, plus extra for brushing
150g (5½oz) egg (about 3 medium eggs), at room temperature
80g (scant ½ cup) light soft brown sugar
⅛ tsp salt
160g (⅔ cup) whole milk
150g (1 cup plus 2 tbsp) chestnut flour
1½ tsp baking powder

1. Set the shelf in the lower half of the oven and preheat it to 180°C/350°F/Gas mark 4. Line a 12-hole muffin tray with muffin cases or, if baking as mini-cakes, chill the moulds in the fridge for 5 minutes, then brush the cavities carefully with melted butter.
2. Put the chocolate and butter in a heatproof bowl (preferably metal). Place the bowl over a saucepan of gently simmering water, ensuring that the water does not reach the bottom of the bowl. Stir with a silicone spatula until the chocolate has completely melted and incorporated the butter. Set aside to cool.
3. Add the eggs, sugar and salt to a bowl large enough to accommodate all the ingredients and whisk with a handheld electric whisk (or use a stand mixer) at high speed until the sugar has completely dissolved and the mixture is pale and fluffy; it will take about 3–4 minutes. Lower the speed to medium and slowly trickle the melted chocolate into the bowl, followed by the milk. Keep whisking for a further minute until the liquids are fully incorporated.
4. Sift the flour and baking powder into the bowl and whisk again at low speed until smooth, with no lumps of flour. The mixture will be rather liquid, almost like a pancake batter. Spoon the batter evenly into the moulds, filling them up to two-thirds and bake for 20 minutes if making cupcakes or 12–13 minutes if making cakelets. A skewer inserted in the deepest part of one of the cakes must come out clean. Leave in the tins to cool for at least 5 minutes.
5. Transfer the cupcakes to a wire rack to cool completely. If making cakelets, invert the tin, tap out the cakes and cover with a clean tea towel (dish towel) while they cool. Tortine castagne e cioccolato keep for up to 3 days under a cake dome.

gluten-free   **PREP TIME:** 25 minutes   **BAKING TIME:** 12–13 or 20 minutes, depending on size   **BAKING TEMPERATURE:** 180°C/350°F/Gas mark 4

PLUMCAKES

Rum cakes

Odd as it sounds, in Italian, plumcake (pronounced 'ploomkayk' with the thickest Italian accent you can muster) is not a cake made with plums. Italians refer to most cakes baked in loaf tins, especially those that include spirit-soaked dried fruit, as 'plumcakes'. This is probably because the oldest versions of this cake were based on British bakes made with prunes, and over time the meaning of the name extended to similarly shaped cakes.

My recipe is based on my dad's family classic: it was one of my mum's favourites, and my dad obliged, baking it quite regularly. Many of my breakfast caffè lattes have been made sweeter by slices of rich plumcake...

Dark rum and dried fruit are the key flavours of these cakes, and I like to use lots. My favourite combination includes dried apricots, mixed candied peel, dried cherries and sultanas (golden raisins), but you can modulate the mix to suit your own taste. I bake mine in paper loaf cases to keep them in the traditional shape, but you can use paper-lined muffin tins too – in this case, bake them for 25–27 minutes only.

MAKES 12

for 125ml (4fl oz) mini loaf cases, 8 x 4 x 4cm (3¼ x 1½ x 1½in)

300g (10½oz) dried apricots, mixed candied peel (page 150), dried cherries and sultanas (golden raisins) in roughly equal amounts
100g (scant ½ cup) dark rum
250g (1 cup plus 2 tbsp) unsalted butter, softened and diced
250g (1¼ cups) dark soft brown sugar
2 tsp vanilla bean paste
¼ tsp salt
250g (9oz) egg (about 5 medium eggs), at room temperature
zest of 1 unwaxed organic lemon
250g (1¾ cups plus 2 tbsp) soft wheat 00 flour or plain (all-purpose) flour
1 tsp baking powder

1. Set the shelf in the middle part of the oven and preheat it to 180°C/350°F/Gas mark 4. Dice the larger fruits like apricots and candied peel so that each piece is no larger than 5mm (¼in). Put the dried fruit and candied peel in a small microwave-safe bowl, add the rum and microwave for about 1 minute, until just warm to the touch. Stir well, cover with a saucer and set aside to soak.

2. Put the butter, sugar, vanilla and salt in the bowl of a stand mixer with the paddle attachment and cream the mixture at high speed until light and fluffy; it will take about 5 minutes. With the mixer running, add the eggs, one a time, allowing each one to be fully incorporated before adding the next. Use a silicone spatula to scrape down the sides of the bowl throughout the process, as necessary.

3. Mix in the lemon zest then take the bowl off the mixer and sift in the flour and baking powder. Return to the mixer and mix again at the lowest speed until the flour is just incorporated.

4. Scoop about a quarter of the soaked fruit from its bowl with a slotted spoon, letting any liquid drain back into the bowl, and set it aside. Add the remaining soaked fruit and rum to the batter and fold it in gently until it is evenly distributed.

5. Divide the batter evenly between the mini loaf cases, filling them up to 1cm (½in) from the rim. Gently tap the cases on the worktop to dispel big air pockets and level out the tops with the back of a spoon. Scatter the reserved drained fruit over the cakes, arrange the cases on a baking tray and bake for 32–34 minutes, or until the tops are golden brown and a skewer inserted in the middle of one comes out clean. Plumcakes keep for up to 3 days under a cake dome.

nut-free   **PREP TIME:** 25 minutes   **TOTAL BAKING TIME:** 32–34 minutes   **BAKING TEMPERATURE:** 180°C/350°F/Gas mark 4

nut-free

PREP TIME: 45 minutes, plus resting time

TOTAL BAKING TIME: 26–28 minutes

BAKING TEMPERATURE: 180°C/350°F/Gas mark 4

Rapallo, a beautiful coastal town in Liguria, claims to be the birthplace of gobeletti, or cubeletti. These dainty pastries with scalloped edges are very common around Genoa and Savona and have been enjoyed by Ligurians since the mid-nineteenth century, historically for celebrations in honour of Saint Agatha.

Originally filled with quince compote, these days they are often made with apples. I like to use sweet apples like Gala or Golden Delicious, but any variety would do as long as it is not too soft and watery. I make the casings with my quick version of shortcrust pastry, ready in less than 5 minutes; you can literally prepare them in no time if you decide to fill them with ready-made jam: apricot, peach or plum make excellent fillings.

Gobeletti are deliciously crunchy when warm, but I prefer to enjoy them the next day, when the flavours fully mature and the pastry is softened up by the juices of the fruit.

MAKES 12

for 6.5-cm (2½-in)
diameter mini-tartlet
moulds or a 12-hole
muffin tray

For the pastry
100g (scant ½ cup)
unsalted butter, at room
temperature, plus extra
for greasing
100g (½ cup) caster
(superfine) sugar
50g (1¾oz) egg (about
1 medium egg),
at room temperature
1 tsp vanilla bean paste
zest of 1 unwaxed
organic lemon
⅛ tsp salt
250g (1¾ cups plus 2 tbsp)
soft wheat 00 flour or
plain (all-purpose) flour,
plus extra for dusting
icing (confectioner's)
sugar, for dusting

For the filling
400g (14oz) sweet apples
(about 3 medium fruits)
50g (¼ cup) caster
(superfine) sugar
3 tbsp freshly squeezed
lemon juice (about
1 lemon)

1. Put the butter, sugar, egg, vanilla, lemon zest and salt in the bowl of a food processor and blitz until fully combined as a homogeneous cream. Transfer the mixture to a large bowl and add the flour. Combine by hand until the pastry comes together in a soft and smooth dough. Wrap in cling film and chill it in the fridge for at least 30 minutes.

2. Meanwhile peel, core and finely dice the apples, so that the pieces are no larger than 2cm (¾in). Put the diced fruit in a small pan with the sugar and lemon juice. Cook, covered, for 10–15 minutes over a moderate heat until the fruit has softened and it looks translucent. Take it off the heat and, while it is still warm, mash it roughly with a fork or a potato masher. The texture should be creamy with some pieces of fruit. Set aside to cool.

3. Set the shelf in the lowest position of the oven and preheat it to 180°C/350°F/ Gas mark 4. Grease the moulds and dust with flour, tapping off any excess.

4. Lightly dust the worktop with flour and roll out the dough to a thickness of 5mm (¼in). Cut twelve 8cm (3¼in) diameter discs with a pastry cutter or with the rim of a cup and fit them snugly in the moulds. Trim off any excess pastry by sliding the back of a knife along the rim of the mould. Spoon ½ tablespoon of cool apple compote in each tartlet.

5. Rework and reroll the offcuts of the pastry, cut another twelve 7cm (2¾in) diameter discs and use them to top the tartlets: place the discs over the compote, press down gently to expel any trapped air, then seal and trim the edges by gently pinching the pastry against the rim of the mould. Cut two slits in the lids with a sharp knife.

6. Arrange the moulds in a baking tray and bake for 26–28 minutes or until the edges of the pastry are just starting to brown. Leave the tartlets to cool in their cases until just warm, then gently unmould by turning them out onto your hand. Arrange them and dust with a light coating of icing sugar. Gobeletti can be served warm or at room temperature. They are best eaten within a day of baking, but can keep for up to 3 days under a cake dome.

CROSTATINE AL MARZAPANE
Marzipan tartlets

Orange and almond are popular flavours in many traditional bakes from southern Italy where fields packed with these trees are a familiar sight. Conveniently, those flavours go brilliantly well together, and the combination is often found in many family bakes. In my tartlets, the bitterness of orange marmalade is balanced by the sweetness of marzipan: the result is a triumph of Mediterranean fragrance in every bite. These tartlets are made with the simplest and quickest shortcrust pastry: all you need is a food processor, a bowl and... less than 5 minutes. The baking powder is optional: I prefer to add it for a softer and crumblier pastry, but you can omit it for a crisper texture. They can be baked in individual tartlet moulds or in a 12-hole muffin tray.

MAKES 12

for 7-cm (2¾-in) diameter
  tartlet moulds or
  a 12-hole muffin tray

For the pastry
100g (scant ½ cup)
  unsalted butter, at room
  temperature, plus extra
  for greasing
100g (½ cup) caster
  (superfine) sugar
50g (1¾oz) egg (about
  1 medium egg), at
  room temperature
1 tsp baking powder (optional)
zest of 1 unwaxed
  organic orange
⅛ tsp salt
250g (1¾ cups plus 2 tbsp)
  soft wheat 00 flour or
  plain (all-purpose) flour,
  plus extra for dusting

For the marzipan
130g (about 1 cup) whole
  blanched almonds
100g (½ cup) caster
  (superfine) sugar
1 tsp baking powder
35g (1¼oz) egg white (about
  1 medium egg white)
½ tsp natural almond extract
zest of 1 unwaxed
  organic lemon

For the assembly
120g (4¼oz) orange
  marmalade
1 beaten egg yolk,
  for brushing
25g (about ¼ cup)
  flaked almonds

1. For the pastry, place the butter, sugar, egg, baking powder (if using), orange zest and salt in the bowl of a food processor and blitz until fully combined as a homogeneous cream. Transfer the mixture to a large bowl and add the flour. Combine by hand until the pastry comes together in a soft and smooth dough. Wrap it in cling film and chill in the fridge for at least 30 minutes.

2. Meanwhile for the marzipan, blitz the almonds with sugar and baking powder in a food processor until the mixture has the texture of coarse sand. It will take less than a minute: do not worry about the odd little fleck of unground almond as it will add a pleasant bite to the filling. Add the egg white, almond extract and lemon zest and blitz again until the mixture comes together (about 20–30 seconds).

3. Set the shelf in the lowest position of the oven and preheat it to 180°C/350°F/Gas mark 4. Grease the moulds and dust them with flour, tapping off any excess.

4. Lightly dust the worktop with flour and roll out the dough to a thickness of 5mm (¼in). Cut twelve 8-cm (3¼-in) diameter discs with a pastry cutter or use the rim of a cup and fit them snugly in the moulds. Any leftover pastry can be rolled and cut into cookies or wrapped in cling film and frozen.

5. Warm the marmalade in the microwave for about 30 seconds, then add a teaspoonful to each tartlet. Wet your hands, take a tablespoonful of marzipan, roll it into a ball between your hands and pat it down on the palm of one hand to make a small circle, then place it on the marmalade in the first tartlet. Repeat with the rest of the marzipan, always keeping your hands wet, until you have covered all the tartlets. Brush the marzipan with egg yolk and sprinkle a small pinch of flaked almonds on each tartlet.

6. Arrange the moulds in a baking tray and bake for 20–22 minutes, until the edges of the pastry are just starting to brown and the marzipan is golden. Leave the tartlets in their cases until just warm, then gently unmould by turning them out onto your hand. Crostatine al marzapane keep for up to a week under a cake dome.

PREP TIME: 25 minutes,
plus resting time

TOTAL BAKING TIME:
20–22 minutes

BAKING TEMPERATURE:
180°C/350°F/Gas mark 4

Gianduja fondant

Usually referred to in Italian as cuore morbido, or 'soft heart', because of their creamy, velvety core, chocolate fondants, also known as lava cakes, or molten chocolate cakes, took the baking world by storm only a few years ago.

My take on this popular cake calls for my beloved gianduja flavour, the key ingredient being hazelnut butter: a thick purée made exclusively with crushed nuts, with no added sugar or oil. It is a relatively expensive ingredient, usually sourced through online retailers, but you can make your own, just by blitzing blanched, toasted hazelnuts in a food processor on full speed until they have been crushed to a smooth pulp.

The batter can be prepared a day in advance, poured in the moulds and stored in the fridge, ready for baking just before serving. It can also be frozen and thawed overnight in the fridge. You can use metal moulds and turn out the fondants onto plates or bake them and serve them directly in ceramic ramekins. In this latter case, bake them for 2 minutes longer and wait 5 minutes before serving.

The recipe is relatively easy and quite forgiving, yet the result is worthy of the most upmarket restaurant menu. Served still warm, next to a scoop of ice cream or crème fraîche, it is the perfect end to a romantic dinner.

MAKES 6

for 175ml (5½fl oz) metal pudding moulds or ceramic ramekins

unsweetened cocoa powder, for dusting
90g (3¼oz) dark chocolate chips, or bar broken into small pieces (50–55% cocoa solids)
120g (½ cup) unsalted butter, plus extra for greasing
40g (3 tbsp) hazelnut butter (see introduction)
150g (5½oz) egg (about 3 medium eggs)
100g (½ cup) caster (superfine) sugar
⅛ tsp salt
100g (¾ cup) soft wheat 00 flour or plain (all-purpose) flour
30g (¼ cup) toasted chopped hazelnuts, plus extra for sprinkling

1. Grease the moulds with butter and dust them with cocoa powder, tapping off any excess.
2. Add the chocolate, butter and hazelnut butter to a heatproof bowl (preferably metal) and place it over a saucepan of gently simmering water, making sure that the water does not reach the bottom of the bowl. Melt the mixture, stirring occasionally, then set aside to cool. Avoid melting the mixture in the microwave as the hazelnut butter may burn.
3. Put the eggs, sugar and salt in a bowl large enough to accommodate all the ingredients and whisk them at high speed with a handheld electric whisk (or use a stand mixer) until the mixture has doubled in volume and looks pale and frothy. It will take 6–8 minutes. Still whisking, slowly trickle in the chocolate and hazelnut mixture. Sift the flour into the bowl and whisk at low speed until the batter looks smooth and lump-free. Fold in the chopped hazelnuts.
4. Spoon or pour the batter into the moulds, filling them just over half-way. Each mould will contain about 100g (3½oz) of batter. Chill the batter in the fridge and, when ready to serve, set the shelf in the middle of the oven and preheat it to 200°C/400°F/Gas mark 6. Arrange the moulds in a baking tray and, when the oven is at temperature, bake for 11 minutes (13, if using ceramic ramekins), or until the fondants have puffed up a little, forming a thin and dull crust on top. They should be still slightly wobbly when shaken. Take them out of the oven and let them rest for 4 minutes (5, if using ceramic ramekins). If using metal moulds, place an upturned small plate on top of the mould and flip it over quickly. The fondant will drop out effortlessly. Sprinkle with chopped hazelnuts before serving. Cuore morbido al gianduja must be served immediately while still warm.

TORTINE ALLA POLENTA

Polenta cakelets

As the name suggests, the ingredients for these golden cakelets include cornmeal, the same used for making polenta, a traditional dish rooted in the culture of most northern regions of Italy. Despite such a rustic addition, these cakelets are exceptionally soft and airy. The inebriating orange fragrance is the dominant flavour, matched perfectly by the sweet chocolate coating. They do come with a health warning though: once you taste the first, it will be really hard to stop...

When buying the cornmeal, avoid any pre-cooked or 'express' polenta, and only use raw, finely ground cornmeal. I bake my cakelets in mini-cake moulds, but they can also be baked in a conventional 12-hole muffin tin as cupcakes.

MAKES 12

For the cupcakes
120g (4¼oz) egg (about 2 large eggs), at room temperature
100g (½ cup) caster (superfine) sugar
1 tsp vanilla bean paste
⅛ tsp salt
80g (⅓ cup) unsalted butter, plus extra for greasing
zest of 1 unwaxed organic orange
40g (8 tsp) freshly squeezed orange juice
½ tsp natural orange extract
100g (¾ cup) soft wheat 00 flour or plain (all-purpose) flour, plus extra for dusting
¾ tsp baking powder
50g (⅓ cup) finely ground cornmeal (polenta)

For the coating
200g (7oz) dark chocolate chips, or bar broken into small pieces (50–55% cocoa solids)
30g (2 tbsp plus 1 tsp) vegetable oil (preferably corn or sunflower)
1 unwaxed organic orange

1. Grease the moulds or muffin tin well with butter and dust with flour, tapping out the excess. Set the shelf in the middle of the oven and preheat it to 170°C/340°F/Gas mark 3½.

2. Add the eggs, sugar, vanilla and salt to the bowl of a stand mixer fitted with the whisk attachment and whip the mixture for 6–8 minutes at high speed until it doubles in volume and is pale and frothy. Meanwhile, put the butter in a small microwave-safe bowl and melt it: 40 seconds in the microwave should be enough. Set aside to cool. When the egg mixture is light and airy, add the orange zest, juice and extract, then gently whisk to incorporate them.

3. Sift the flour and baking powder into the mixture, add the cornmeal and fold in very gently with a silicone spatula until fully combined. Finally, add the cooled melted butter and fold it into the batter. Ensure that the butter is fully incorporated and it is not pooling by scraping the sides and bottom of the bowl thoroughly with the spatula.

4. Spoon the batter into the moulds filling them to 5mm (¼in) from the rim. Bake immediately for 14–15 minutes, or until the tops are a light caramel colour and a skewer inserted into the deepest part of one comes out clean. Let the cakelets cool in the moulds for 5 minutes, then turn out onto a wire rack to cool completely. Once cool, chill in the fridge for 30 minutes.

5. Meanwhile, put the chocolate and oil in a small bowl and microwave it for 1 minute, then stir well and microwave in 10-second bursts, stirring well between subsequent bursts until completely melted. Set aside to cool for a few minutes. Place the rack with the cakelets on a sheet of baking paper. Holding one upside-down, dip its top half into the melted chocolate, then place it back on the rack, allowing the excess chocolate to drip onto the baking paper. Repeat until all cakelets are coated. Zest the orange with a vegetable peeler and slice the zest into thin strips. Decorate the cakelets with the strips while the chocolate is still warm. Once it has set, transfer to a serving tray. Tortine alla polenta keep for up to 4 days under a cake dome.

nut-free

PREP TIME: 30 minutes, plus setting time

TOTAL BAKING TIME: 14–15 minutes

BAKING TEMPERATURE: 170°C/340°F/Gas mark 3½

PARROZZINI

Parrozzini are my single-serving version of parrozzo, a traditional Christmas bake from Abruzzo. The recipe is just over a century old and it was conceived in the coastal city of Pescara to create a cake that resembled a loaf of local rustic bread.

   The flavour of parrozzini is unmistakably and intensely almondy: whole, unblanched nuts should be used for the best flavour and texture. Ready-ground almonds are a quicker option but they tend to make a drier, less flavoursome sponge. The ingredients should ideally include a few bitter almonds or apricot kernels to give it further depth, but this is not critical.

   I have added butter and liqueur to the traditional recipe to make the sponge softer, but the liqueur can be replaced with freshly squeezed orange juice for a non-alcoholic version. The traditional shape is half-sphere, and I bake mine in silicone moulds, which make releasing the little cakes easy. However, they are as easily baked in conventional muffin tins. Parrozzini go very well with a dollop of mascarpone sauce (page 175) or spread with a generous layer of cherry compote.

MAKES 12

for 7cm (2¼in) diameter
   hemisphere moulds

For the sponge
130g (about 1 cup) whole
   unblanched almonds
   (possibly including
   5–10 apricot kernels)
80g (⅓ cup) unsalted
   butter, plus extra for
   greasing
60g (2¼oz) egg yolk and
   140g (5oz) egg white
   (about 4 medium eggs),
   at room temperature
130g (⅔ cup) caster
   (superfine) sugar
1 tsp vanilla bean paste
⅛ tsp salt
zest of 1 unwaxed organic
   orange
30g (2 tbsp) sambuca or
   amaretto liqueur
1 tsp natural almond
   extract
100g (⅔ cup) semolina,
   plus extra for dusting
⅛ tsp cream of tartar or
   ½ tsp lemon juice

1. Grease 12 hemisphere moulds with butter: if using silicone moulds, this will be enough, but for metal ones, lightly dust them with semolina too. Set the shelf in the lower half of the oven and preheat it to 160°C/320°F/Gas mark 3.

2. Grind the almonds with the apricot kernels (if using) in a food processor until they have the texture of fine sand. Set aside. (If using ready-ground almonds, skip this step entirely.)

3. Put the butter in a small microwave-safe bowl and melt it: 30–40 seconds in the microwave should be enough. Set aside to cool.

4. Put the egg yolks, half the sugar, the vanilla and salt in a medium bowl and whisk with a handheld electric whisk on high speed until the mixture doubles in size and looks pale and frothy; it will take 6–8 minutes. With the whisk on medium speed, stream the melted, cooled butter into the mixture then add the orange zest, liqueur and almond extract, and keep whisking until fully combined. Gently fold in the ground almonds and semolina using a silicone spatula until just incorporated: do not overmix to avoid deflating the batter.

5. Thoroughly wash and dry the whisk. Put the egg whites and cream of tartar or lemon juice into a clean bowl, preferably metal, ceramic or glass, and whisk at medium speed until the whisk leaves visible marks on the egg-white surface; it will take about 1 minute. Still whisking, gradually add the remaining sugar to form a stiff but supple meringue; it will take about 2 minutes.

6. Add the meringue to the batter in three goes, folding it in gently after each addition until no more white streaks are visible. Pour or spoon the batter, dividing it evenly between the 12 moulds and filling them to within 1cm (½in) from the rim. Immediately place in the oven and bake for about 30 minutes until a skewer inserted into the middle of one cake comes out clean. The sponge should feel firm and springy and just very lightly browned.

Recipe continues overleaf

For the coating
400g (14oz) dark chocolate chips, or bar broken into small pieces (50–55% cocoa solids)
60g (¼ cup) vegetable oil (preferably corn or sunflower)
gold leaf (optional)

7. Allow the parrozzini to cool in the moulds for 5 minutes, then turn them out onto a wire rack to cool completely. Once cool, chill in the fridge for at least 30 minutes.

8. Meanwhile, put the chocolate and oil in a small bowl and microwave for 1 minute, then stir well and keep microwaving in 10-second bursts, stirring well between each burst, until completely melted. Take the parrozzini out of the fridge and set them on a wire rack placed over a sheet of baking paper. Pour or spoon the melted chocolate over each one, allowing the excess to drip onto the baking paper. Once they are all coated, gently tap the rack on the worktop – this will even out the coating. Leave the chocolate to set, then transfer the parrozzini to a serving tray and decorate with a sliver of gold leaf (if using). They will keep for up to a week under a cake dome.

Fruit tartlets

I am partial to a glistening fruit tart, especially in the warmer months, when the fruit is ripe and at its sweetest. Admittedly, preparing pastry, crème pât and arranging the fruit in a regular pattern is not exactly a quick job, so I have come up with a cheat's version of the classic fruit tart, that brings together the same fresh, fruity flavours in a much quicker and easier bake.

Tartellette alla frutta are based on a simple, soft and citrussy sponge, topped with a colourful array of scattered fruit, brushed with a honey glaze. I usually go for a combination of kiwi, mango, grapes and berries, but any soft fruit would do; just keep it colourful and avoid watery varieties like watermelon or pear, and ones that brown easily like apple or banana.

Tartellette alla frutta are baked in tartlet tins, but they can easily be morphed into cupcakes and baked in a conventional muffin tray instead. The tanginess of yogurt sauce (page 173) complements the sweetness of the fruit brilliantly but, for a more decadent dessert, go for a generous dollop of mascarpone sauce (page 175).

MAKES 8

for 10cm (4in) diameter
    tartlet cases

butter, for greasing
300g (10½oz) mixed
    fresh fruit
100g (3½oz) egg (about
    2 medium eggs), at room
    temperature
100g (½ cup) caster
    (superfine) sugar
1 tsp vanilla bean paste
⅛ tsp salt
30g (2 tbsp plus 1 tsp)
    vegetable oil (preferably
    corn or sunflower)
140g (scant ¾ cup)
    double (heavy) cream
    (45–50% fat)
160g (scant 1¼ cups) soft
    wheat 00 flour or plain
    (all-purpose) flour,
    plus extra for dusting
1 tsp baking powder
1 tsp ground ginger
zest of 1 organic
    unwaxed lemon
40g (8 tsp) clear honey
2 tbsp freshly squeezed
    lemon juice

1. Set the shelf in the middle of the oven and preheat it to 180°C/350°F/Gas mark 4. Grease the tartlet cases with butter and dust them with flour. Tap out the excess flour and set aside.

2. Wash, drain and pat the fruit dry. Peel, if necessary, and slice larger fruits but leave smaller berries whole. Set aside.

3. Put the eggs, sugar, vanilla and salt in a large bowl and whisk with a handheld electric whisk (or use a stand mixer) at high speed, until the sugar has completely dissolved and the mixture is pale and fluffy; it will take about 3–4 minutes. Still whisking, slowly trickle first the oil then the cream into the bowl, and whisk for a further minute until the liquids are fully incorporated.

4. Sift the flour, baking powder and ginger into the bowl, add the lemon zest and whisk again at low speed until the batter is smooth, without any lumps of flour.

5. Pour or spoon the batter, dividing it evenly between the 8 tartlet cases, filling them to half-way up. Top the tartlets with fruit, scattering the pieces randomly. Bake for 24–26 minutes, or until golden on top.

6. Leave the tartlets in their cases until just warm, then gently unmould by turning them out onto your hand. While the tartlets are still warm, put the honey and lemon juice into a small pan, bring to a gentle simmer over a medium heat, then brush the syrup over the tartlets. Tartellette alla frutta keep for up to 3 days under a cake dome.

PREP TIME: 30 minutes,
plus cooling time

TOTAL BAKING TIME:
24–26 minutes

BAKING TEMPERATURE:
180°C/350°F/Gas mark 4

nut-free

FETTA AL LATTE

Milky slice

Fetta al latte is a popular snack created by Kinder in 1991 and is loved in Italy. Two layers of soft cocoa sponge sandwich a generous cream filling, which must be almost as thick as the sponge itself to deliver a simple, chocolatey cake with a fresh and fulfilling centre.

The sponge is a variation on pasta biscotto, a flexible and soft cake made without any raising agent and baked relatively thin. It is very easy to make but you must whip the eggs long enough to incorporate loads of air. Fold in the flour and cocoa very gently to keep it lofty and do not overbake it: as soon as the cake passes the skewer test, take it out of the oven.

These milky slices are bound to become a hit with the kids and will have everybody licking their fingers at the next birthday party.

MAKES 8

for a 25 x 38cm
(10 x 15in) Swiss roll
tin (jelly roll pan)

butter, for greasing
200g (7oz) egg (about
4 medium eggs), at
room temperature
100g (½ cup) caster
(superfine) sugar
1 tsp vanilla bean paste
40g (3 tbsp) vegetable
oil (preferably corn or
sunflower)
70g (½ cup) soft wheat
00 flour or plain
(all-purpose) flour
20g (3 tbsp) unsweetened
cocoa powder
150g (generous ½ cup)
whipping (heavy) cream
(35–40% fat)
100g (scant ½ cup)
mascarpone
20g (generous 1 tbsp)
clear honey
50g (generous ⅓ cup)
icing (confectioner's)
sugar

1. Set the shelf in the middle of the oven and preheat it to 200°C/400°F/ Gas mark 6. Grease the tin with butter and line it with baking paper.
2. Put the eggs, sugar and vanilla in the bowl of a stand mixer and whisk at high speed until the mixture has at least tripled in volume and it looks stiff and full of air; it will take 8–10 minutes. Still whisking, slowly trickle the oil into the bowl, and keep whisking for a further minute until the oil is fully incorporated.
3. Take the bowl off the mixer, sift in the flour and cocoa powder, and fold them in very gently with a silicone spatula until the mixture is an even chocolate colour, without any streaks. Make sure to scrape the bottom of the bowl well, as that is where the dry ingredients tend to clump. Pour the batter into the lined tin, level it out with an offset spatula or a straight, long knife and place immediately in the oven. Bake for about 12 minutes or until a skewer inserted into the cake comes out clean.
4. Meanwhile, prepare a wire rack and a sheet of baking paper slightly larger than the tin. For the next step it is advisable to wear oven mitts as the cake needs to be handled while piping hot. Take the cake out of the oven, cover it with the sheet of baking paper and place the wire rack, upside down, over it. Turn the whole stack (tin, cake, baking paper and wire rack) over, so that the cake drops onto the lined wire rack. Place the stack on the worktop and remove the tin. Gently peel off the baking paper on which the cake was baked then cover the sponge with a clean tea towel (dish towel) and leave to cool completely.
5. Meanwhile, put the cream, mascarpone, honey and icing sugar in a medium bowl and whisk to stiff peaks. Do not overmix or the cream will curdle: stop as soon as the surface changes from shiny to dull.
6. Position the cake on the worktop with a long side facing you and cut it into two lengthways, so you now have two halves, each about 38 x 12cm (15 x 4½in). Spoon the filling onto one half and spread it evenly with an offset spatula or a straight-edge knife.

 nut-free

PREP TIME: 35 minutes, plus chilling time

TOTAL BAKING TIME: 12 minutes

BAKING TEMPERATURE: 200°C/400°F/Gas mark 6

7. Place the second half of the sponge over the filling and place the
   assembled cake in the freezer for at least 40 minutes or until the filling
   has hardened slightly. Remove the cake from the freezer, trim off the four
   edges to neaten the cake and slice it into eight rectangles about 10 x 4cm
   (4 x 1½in) each. Fetta al latte should be served chilled; the slices keep for
   up to 3 days, wrapped in cling film and stored in the fridge. They can also
   be frozen, individually wrapped in cling film, and defrosted (still wrapped)
   a few hours before serving.

BISCUITS COOKIES

Cantucci	92
Frollini di riso	94
Abbracci	96
Pinolini	98
Castagnotti	100
Zaleti	102
Biscotti al limone	104
Pistacchini	106
Nocciolatini	108
Baci di dama	110
Krumiri	113
Biscotti noci e marmellata	116
Settembrini	118
Pizzicotti al mandarino	120
Nidi di cocco all'albicocca	122
Lingue di gatto	124
Pasticcini al caffè	126
Biscotti all'amarena	128
Susamelli	130
Pasticcini di frolla montata	132
Roccocò	136
Mostaccioli	138

&

CANTUCCI

Almond biscuits

Few biscuits are as iconic as cantucci: well known the world over, these Tuscan delicacies were first conceived in the sixteenth century, with the current recipe eventually developed about 300 years later in Prato. Cantucci are fatless, they are baked twice to dry out completely, and as such are probably one of the few rightful 'biscuits' (biscotto literally means 'cooked twice'). Several versions, with minor variations, are common across central Italy under a variety of different names, including tozzetti or scroccadenti (meaning teeth crackers!).

The recipe could not be simpler; it requires no technical skill and it only calls for everyday cupboard staples. I have used exclusively almonds in my recipe to keep it closer to the original, but they can be partially or entirely swapped for your favourite nut: hazelnuts and pistachios work particularly well.

Cantucci are often served alongside an espresso, but it is when they are dunked in a glass of vin santo that they are elevated to a truly different level: taste the pair together and you will experience one of the simplest yet most memorable gifts of Italian baking.

MAKES 24

50g (1¾oz) egg (about 1 medium egg)
120g (scant ⅔ cup) caster (superfine) sugar
1 tsp vanilla bean paste
zest of 1 unwaxed organic lemon
zest of 1 unwaxed organic orange
⅛ tsp salt
140g (1 cup) soft wheat 00 flour or plain (all-purpose) flour, plus extra for dusting
½ tsp baking powder
100g (about ¾ cup) whole unblanched almonds

1. Set the shelf in the middle of the oven and preheat it to 180°C/350°F/Gas mark 4. Line a baking tray with baking paper or a silicone mat.
2. Put the egg, sugar, vanilla, citrus zest and salt in a bowl large enough to accommodate all the ingredients and lightly whisk them by hand, just long enough to combine. Sift in the flour and baking powder and combine, first with a spoon, then by hand until the mixture comes together as a soft dough. Add the almonds and work the dough to incorporate them. Turn the dough onto a lightly floured worktop and divide it into two halves, shape each half as a large sausage, no more than 3cm (1¼in) thick, then place them on the lined baking sheet.
3. Bake for 23–25 minutes until the sausages have puffed up and the tops are lightly browned. Take them out of the oven and lower the oven temperature to 150°C/300°F/Gas mark 2. Allow the biscuits to cool for 5 minutes on the baking sheet and, when firm enough to handle, slice them diagonally into 2-cm (¾-in) wide slices with a sharp, serrated knife.
4. Place the still-warm slices sideways back onto the baking sheet and bake for a further 10 minutes, turning them over midway to ensure an even bake. Leave the biscuits to cool for a few minutes on the baking sheet, then transfer them to a wire rack to cool completely. Cantucci keep for up to a month in an airtight container.

dairy-free

PREP TIME: 20 minutes, plus cooling time

TOTAL BAKING TIME: 33–35 minutes

BAKING TEMPERATURE: 180°C/350°F/Gas mark 4

FROLLINI DI RISO

Rice biscuits

The traditional Italian breakfast at home consists of a bowl of caffè latte and a handful of dry biscuits, specifically made for dunking. Frollini are the simplest version of such biscuits and are so popular that they take over entire aisles in Italian supermarkets, articulated in a vast array of flavours and shapes.

Frollini are the perfect family recipe: they take no longer than 15 minutes to prepare, are very simple to shape and involve no waste or reworking of the dough. Although typically served for breakfast, I find that the sweetness of these biscuits is simply unbeatable when dunked in hot, unsweetened espresso any time of the day. For a luscious, indulgent treat, pair them with milk chocolate sauce (page 173).

My gluten-free version calls for white rice flour; make sure you do not use the glutinous type as it would alter the texture and taste. Rice flour delivers an extremely delicate and crumbly texture, although plain (all-purpose) wheat flour can be used as well, to make frollini with more body and structure.

MAKES 16

200g (scant 1½ cups) white rice flour
90g (⅔ cup) icing (confectioner's) sugar
¼ tsp salt
½ tsp baking powder
50g (1¾oz) whole egg (about 1 medium egg)
2 tsp vanilla bean paste
70g (⅓ cup) unsalted butter, softened and diced

1. Add the flour, sugar, salt and baking powder to the bowl of a stand mixer and mix well with a spoon until fully combined. Add the egg and vanilla and start the mixer, using the paddle attachment, on a medium speed, working until the mixture looks fine and sandy. Add the butter and keep mixing until fully incorporated; the mixture will look loose and flaky.

2. Turn out the dough onto a clean and dry worktop, pat it down with the palm of your hand and, using a straight-edge scraper, lift one side and fold it over. Repeat the patting and folding a couple of times until the dough comes together as a coherent mass. Shape it as a brick with 4 x 6cm (1½ x 2½in) sides, wrap in cling film and chill for at least 1 hour.

3. When ready to bake, set the shelf in the middle of the oven and preheat it to 180°C/350°F/Gas mark 4. Line a baking sheet with baking paper or a silicone mat.

4. Take the dough out of the fridge and, using a sharp, straight-edge knife, slice it into 16 rectangles, each about 1cm (½in) thick. Arrange the biscuits on the lined sheet and texture the surface with the prongs of a fork, or you can use a cookie stamp, if you have one.

5. Bake for 13–15 minutes or until the bottom edges start to turn golden. Do not be tempted to touch or move the biscuits when they come out of the oven as they are extremely crumbly when hot. Instead, slide the baking paper onto a wire rack and take them off only when completely cool. Frollini keep for up to a week in an airtight container.

PREP TIME: 15 minutes, plus resting time

TOTAL BAKING TIME: 13–15 minutes

BAKING TEMPERATURE: 180°C/350°F/Gas mark 4

gluten-free, nut-free

ABBRACCI

<u>Hugs</u>

In 1987 Mulino Bianco, a leading Italian producer of baked goods, launched abbracci, a breakfast biscuit shaped as a two-colour ring, where the cocoa- and cream-flavoured halves seem to charmingly 'hug' each other. The name was quite cleverly picked as abbracci means 'hugs' in Italian. They were an immediate success and, a few decades down the line, they have become so popular that you would struggle to find an Italian that does not know them and love them.

The recipe is a simple, buttery and crumbly pastry, half of which is flavoured with cocoa powder. My method makes the process mess-free and straightforward. The result is uncannily similar to the commercial counterpart, and I can guarantee that, once you try them, you will not accept any other biscuit to go with your morning caffè latte.

MAKES 18

100g (scant ½ cup) unsalted butter, softened and diced
100g (generous ¾ cup) icing (confectioner's) sugar
1 tsp vanilla bean paste
small pinch of salt
50g (1¾oz) egg (about 1 medium egg), at room temperature
190g (scant 1½ cups) soft wheat 00 flour or plain (all-purpose) flour
¼ tsp baking powder
15g (2 tbsp) cornflour (cornstarch)
15g (2 tbsp) unsweetened cocoa powder

1. Put the butter, icing sugar, vanilla and salt in the bowl of a stand mixer with a paddle attachment and beat them at high speed until pale and fluffy; it will take about 4–5 minutes. Meanwhile, beat the egg in a cup or a small jug, then add it to the bowl gradually, while still beating at high speed. Sift the flour and baking powder into the bowl and mix on low speed until just combined.

2. Take the bowl off the mixer and divide the mixture equally between two bowls. Add the cornflour to one and the cocoa powder to the other, then gently knead them separately by hand to incorporate the powders. Wrap each dough in a sheet of cling film and chill in the fridge for at least 1 hour. Meanwhile, line a baking sheet with baking paper or a silicone mat.

3. Once the dough has rested, divide each portion into 18 little, evenly sized lumps (they will be about 12g (⅓oz) each). Shape each lump as a 1.5-cm (⅝-in) thick noodle, about 8cm (3¼in) long. Join two noodles, one chocolate, one vanilla, end-to-end to form a two-colour ring. Overlap the ends slightly and press them gently to secure them together. Arrange the biscuits on the lined baking sheet and chill in the fridge for at least 30 minutes.

4. Meanwhile, set the shelf in the middle of the oven and preheat it to 180°C/350°F/Gas mark 4. Once the biscuits have chilled sufficiently, bake them directly from the fridge for 18–20 minutes or until the vanilla portion starts to turn light amber. Allow to cool on the sheet for a few minutes before transferring to a wire rack to cool completely. Abbracci keep for up to a week in an airtight container.

nut-free

PREP TIME: 25 minutes, plus resting and chilling

TOTAL BAKING TIME: 18–20 minutes

BAKING TEMPERATURE: 180°C/350°F/Gas mark 4

PINOLINI
Pine nut cookies

Pinolini are crumbly, crispy cookies traditionally baked in Liguria. The lightly flavoured dough gives the delicate fragrance of pine nuts centre stage. They are an excellent addition to a tray of tea biscuits and keep long enough to be given as a thoughtful present. The recipe is simple and robust enough to be suitable for kids or less experienced bakers.

Pine nuts may release oil when overworked, but this is to be expected and will not compromise the success of the bake. You can swap some of the pine nuts with raisins or chopped dried apricots for a more sophisticated flavour.

MAKES 24

80g (generous ½ cup) pine nuts
220g (1⅔ cups) soft wheat 00 flour or plain (all-purpose) flour, plus extra for dusting
80g (scant ½ cup) caster (superfine) sugar
1 tsp baking powder
⅛ tsp salt
70g (generous ¼ cup) vegetable oil (preferably corn or sunflower)
50g (1¾oz) egg (about 1 medium egg)
1 tsp vanilla bean paste
zest of 1 unwaxed organic orange
icing (confectioner's) sugar, for dusting

1. Set the shelf in the middle of the oven and preheat it to 180°C/350°F/Gas mark 4. Line a baking sheet with baking paper or a silicone mat. Take 50g (scant ½ cup) of the pine nuts, chop them roughly and set aside. Put the remaining pine nuts in a small bowl; they will be used later.
2. Put the flour, sugar, baking powder and salt in a bowl large enough to accommodate all the ingredients and mix with a spoon until fully combined. Make a well in the dry ingredients and add the oil, egg, vanilla and orange zest. Start incorporating the ingredients with the spoon first, then by hand until they come together as a soft, pliable dough.
3. Add the chopped pine nuts to the bowl and mix briefly by hand to incorporate them into the dough. Divide the dough into 24 equal lumps, then roll each lump of dough between the palms of your hands to shape into a ball. Press each one gently into the whole pine nuts set aside earlier, so that a few stick to it: they might need some convincing as the dough is rather oily, so you will have to push the pine nuts gently into it to make them stay. Repeat with all the biscuits, then arrange them on the lined baking sheet and bake for 15–16 minutes. The cookies are done when their bottoms are light brown and the pine nuts start to turn golden.
4. Leave the cookies to cool completely on the baking sheet before taking them off. Transfer them to a serving plate and dust them lightly with icing sugar. Pinolini keep for up to a week in an airtight container.

PREP TIME: 20 minutes   **TOTAL BAKING TIME:** 15–16 minutes   **BAKING TEMPERATURE:** 180°C/350°F/Gas mark 4   dairy-free

CASTAGNOTTI
Chestnut cookies

Saint Martin's Day on the 11th November is a critical milestone in the old rural calendar in many European countries: the grape harvest is over and the freshly crushed fruit starts turning into wine. In Italy, this is celebrated by cheering with vino novello, or new wine, over a good serving of roasted or boiled chestnuts. Their nutty flavour and creamy texture are just perfect to accompany a glass of young red. Castagnotti translate the addictive taste of chestnuts into a fragrant and crumbly cookie, deceptively simple to shape, and with a cunning coating of chocolate that turns them into an irresistibly pretty treat.

The chestnut flour produces a very forgiving dough: it needs to be kneaded for longer than conventional wheat flour to come together and become pliable, but the pastry can be re-rolled as often as needed without ever getting tough.

MAKES 36

100g (¾ cup) soft wheat 00 flour or plain (all-purpose) flour
200g (1½ cups) chestnut flour
100g (½ cup) dark soft brown sugar
1 tsp baking powder
⅛ tsp salt
130g (½ cup plus 1 tbsp) unsalted butter, cold and diced
50g (1¾oz) egg (about 1 medium egg), at room temperature
250g (9oz) dark chocolate chips, or bar broken into small pieces (50–55% cocoa solids)

1. Add both flours, the sugar, baking powder and salt to the bowl of a food processor and stir with a spoon until fully combined. Add the butter and blitz until the mixture resembles sand. Add the egg and blitz again until the mixture resembles soft flakes. Transfer it to a clean and dry worktop and crush it with your hands to bind the flakes together, then pat it down with the palm of your hand. Using a straight-edge scraper, lift one side and fold it over. Repeat the patting and folding a few times until the dough feels smooth and pliable. Flatten to about 2cm (¾in) thickness, wrap in cling film and chill in the fridge for at least 30 minutes.

2. When ready to bake, set the shelf in the middle of the oven and preheat it to 180°C/350°F/Gas mark 4. Line two baking trays with baking paper or silicone mats. Take the dough out of the fridge and roll it out to 8mm (3¼in) thickness over a lightly floured worktop. Cut circles in the dough with a 4cm (1½in) pastry cutter, then arrange them on the lined baking sheets, spacing them 2–3cm (about 1in) apart. Offcuts can be re-worked and re-rolled to make more cookies. Pinch the top of each biscuit to shape them as chestnuts, then bake one tray at a time for about 10 minutes. Allow the cookies to cool on the tray for a couple of minutes before transferring them to a wire rack to cool completely. Keep the baking paper for the next step.

3. Put the chocolate in a small bowl and microwave it for 1 minute, then stir well and keep microwaving it in 10-second bursts, stirring it well between subsequent bursts until completely melted. Set aside to cool for a few minutes. Holding one cookie by the bottom of the chestnut shape, dip it pointed-end first into the chocolate to coat about three-quarters of the cookie. Tilt it from side to side to give the coating a curved edge, then place it on the baking paper to set. Repeat with the rest. Castagnotti keep for up to a week in a biscuit tin.

PREP TIME: 25 minutes, plus resting time

TOTAL BAKING TIME: 20 minutes

BAKING TEMPERATURE: 180°C/350°F/Gas mark 4

ZALETI

Polenta biscuits

The recipe for zaleti dates back to seventeenth-century rural Veneto and Friuli Venezia Giulia, the regions around Venice. The name literally means 'little yellow ones' in the local dialect, clearly referring to their characteristic colour given by the cornmeal used in the dough.

Zaleti are rustic biscuits with a coarse texture, made with ingredients that were easy to source and cheap in north-east Italy back in the day. They can be made with a bowl and a spoon and, although they are typically diamond shaped, you can literally have your kids dropping misshapen lumps of zaleti dough on the baking sheet and they will still turn out pretty and appetising, as long as you do not skimp on the icing sugar!

I like to load mine with a good handful of raisins or dried cherries, especially when properly soaked in good-quality grappa, so give the fruit enough time to plump up in the spirit, ideally overnight. Zaleti marry perfectly with tea, coffee or sweet wine.

MAKES 20

80g (generous ½ cup)
   raisins or dried cherries
30g (2 tbsp) grappa
   or vodka
40g (1½oz) unsalted butter,
   softened and diced
60g (⅓ cup) caster
   (superfine) sugar
⅛ tsp salt
35g (1¼oz) egg yolk (about
   2 medium egg yolks)
1 tsp vanilla bean paste
70g (½ cup) soft wheat
   00 flour or plain (all-
   purpose) flour, plus
   extra for dusting
100g (about ⅔ cup)
   finely ground cornmeal
   (polenta)
icing (confectioner's)
   sugar, for dusting

1. Put the raisins in a small bowl and add the grappa. Cover with a plate and leave to soak for at least 1 hour or, better, overnight.

2. Put the butter, sugar and salt in a bowl large enough to accommodate all the ingredients and cream the mixture with a handheld electric whisk on high speed until pale and fluffy; it will take about 4–5 minutes. (A stand mixer can be used too, but a large paddle attachment might be oversized for such small quantities.) Add the egg yolk and vanilla to the bowl and mix again to incorporate them. Sift the flour into the bowl, add the cornmeal, raisins and their soaking liquid, and mix to combine. Turn out the dough onto a lightly floured worktop and shape it into a 3-cm (1¼-in) thick sausage. The dough will be rather sticky, so a straight-edge scraper will be essential to lift it off the worktop. Wrap in cling film and chill it in the fridge for at least 30 minutes.

3. When ready to bake, line a baking sheet with baking paper or a silicone mat. Set the shelf in the middle of the oven and preheat it to 180°C/350°F/Gas mark 4. Divide the dough into 20 evenly sized lumps, each about 20g (¾oz). Shape each lump as a 1-cm (½in) thick diamond on a lightly floured worktop and place on the lined baking sheet, spaced apart. Bake for 15–17 minutes or until the underside of the biscuits starts to brown. Leave the biscuits on the sheet to cool for a few minutes then transfer them to a wire rack to cool completely. Decorate with a generous dusting of icing sugar before serving. Zaleti keep for up to a week in an airtight container.

PREP TIME: 25 minutes,
plus soaking and resting

TOTAL BAKING TIME:
15–17 minutes

BAKING TEMPERATURE:
180°C/350°F/Gas mark 4

nut-free

Lemon crinkle biscuits

Sicily is the homeland of citrus fruit, and these lemon biscuits come straight from a Sicilian family friend who has been baking them for decades. The double serving of zest means that these biscuits are unapologetically lemony, with an extremely soft and crumbly texture.

Biscotti al limone are great any time of the day but are perfect as elevenses with a good cup of tea. And they are not exclusively for grown-ups: the sweet and tangy flavour makes them ideal treats for the kids' mid-afternoon snack. Needless to say, lemon can be swapped with your favourite citrus fruit: orange will deliver a sweeter flavour, while lime will pack quite a punch!

MAKES 32

120g (½ cup) unsalted butter, softened and diced
120g (⅔ cup) caster (superfine) sugar
¼ tsp salt
50g (1¾oz) egg (about 1 medium egg)
1 tsp vanilla bean paste
zest of 2 unwaxed organic lemons, plus 50g (1¾oz) freshly squeezed juice
1 tsp bicarbonate of soda (baking soda)
300g (2¼ cups) plain (all-purpose) flour
30g (¼ cup) cornflour (cornstarch)
80g (about ⅔ cup) icing (confectioner's) sugar

1. Put the butter, sugar and salt in the bowl of a stand mixer with the paddle attachment and cream the mixture at high speed until pale and fluffy; it will take about 3–4 minutes. Add the egg, vanilla and lemon zest and mix again at high speed until the egg is fully incorporated, scraping down the sides of the bowl with a silicone spatula, if necessary.

2. Sift, in this order: the bicarbonate of soda, flour and cornflour into the bowl, then squeeze 50g (1¾oz) of juice from the zested lemons and add it to the bowl. Mix at low speed until all the ingredients are well combined in a smooth dough. If you add the lemon juice directly to the buttery mix, the mixture might curdle, but keep going and it will come together nicely when adding the flours. The dough will be rather sticky but wrap in cling film and chill it in the fridge for at least 1 hour and it will become much stiffer and more manageable.

3. When ready to bake, set the shelf in the middle of the oven and preheat it to 180°C/350°F/Gas mark 4. Line two baking sheets with baking paper or silicone mats. Put the icing sugar on a plate. Take small lumps of dough, roughly a tablespoonful or about 20g (¾oz), roll them between your hands to shape them as little balls. Roll them very generously in the icing sugar until they are fully coated in a thick layer of sugar, and distribute them across the baking trays, spacing them at least 5cm (2in) apart.

4. Bake one sheet at a time for 12–13 minutes, or until golden cracks appear on the sugared surface of the biscuits. The biscuits are done when the bottoms look golden. Slide the baking paper onto a wire rack and allow the biscuits to cool completely before taking them off the paper. Serve at room temperature. Biscotti al limone keep for up to a week in an airtight container.

PREP TIME: less than 20 minutes, plus resting time

TOTAL BAKING TIME: 24–26 minutes

BAKING TEMPERATURE: 180°C/350°F/Gas mark 4

nut-free

PISTACCHINI

Pistachio biscuits

If you like pistachios, you will love pistacchini: an easy-to-make, buttery and crumbly biscuit based on a simple shortcrust pastry and bursting with warming nuttiness. The original Sicilian recipe uses whole pistachio kernels rather than pre-ground ones, as this is the best way to extract the most intense flavour. Some home bakers are reluctant to grind whole nuts for fear of overheating them but processing them with the flour is a safe option and always works well.

Despite their simplicity, pistacchini are worthy of the most sophisticated patisserie window. Their shape and decoration are a clear reference to pistachios but the white chocolate coating adds a layer of milky sweetness, perfectly matched to the highly aromatic notes of the biscuit.

MAKES 24

100g (¾ cup) unsalted
  pistachio kernels,
  plus 24 whole kernels
  to decorate
250g (1¾ cups plus 2 tbsp)
  soft wheat 00 flour or
  plain (all-purpose) flour
½ tsp baking powder
100g (scant ½ cup)
  unsalted butter,
  softened and diced
120g (⅔ cup) caster
  (superfine) sugar
1 tsp vanilla bean paste
⅛ tsp salt
50g (1¾oz) egg (about
  1 medium egg), at room
  temperature
150g (5½oz) white
  chocolate

1. Put the pistachio kernels, flour and baking powder in the bowl of a food processor and blitz until the mixture has the texture of coarse sand. Set aside. Put the butter, sugar, vanilla and salt in the bowl of a mixer with the paddle attachment and cream the mixture at medium-high speed until soft; it will take about 2 minutes. With the mixer still running, add the egg and mix until fully incorporated. Use a silicone spatula to scrape down the sides of the bowl if needed. Add the pistachio and flour mixture and mix at low speed until it comes together as a soft dough. Wrap in cling film and chill in the fridge for at least 1 hour.

2. When ready to bake, set the shelf just above the middle of the oven and preheat it to 180°C/350°F/Gas mark 4. Line two baking sheets with baking paper or silicone mats. Divide the chilled dough evenly into 24 lumps, each about 25g (1oz). Roll each one into an oval with tapered ends to resemble a pistachio nut. Place them, evenly spaced, on the lined baking sheets, flatten slightly and push a whole pistachio kernel on one end of each biscuit.

3. Bake one tray at a time for 12–13 minutes or until the pointed ends of the biscuits just start to turn amber. Leave the biscuits to cool for a few minutes on the tray, then transfer them to a wire rack to cool completely.

4. Meanwhile, put the chocolate in a small bowl and microwave it for 1 minute, then stir well and keep microwaving it in 10-second bursts, stirring well between subsequent bursts until completely melted. Arrange the pistacchini on a sheet of baking paper, then partially dip them sideways in the melted chocolate to coat about a third of the biscuit. Allow the excess chocolate to drip back into the bowl before returning the pistacchini to the baking paper to set. Pistacchini keep for up to a week in an airtight container.

PREP TIME: 30 minutes,
plus resting time

TOTAL BAKING TIME:
24–26 minutes

BAKING TEMPERATURE:
180°C/350°F/Gas mark 4

Hazelnut biscuits

Nocciolatini are one of the many ways Italians have devised to use the abundance of high-quality hazelnuts that Piedmont produces. These buttery and nutty biscuits have been so successful that they have now spread across the whole country and found their way into many families' recipe books.

The crumbliness of the biscuit complements perfectly the creaminess of the chocolate and hazelnut spread; the warming flavour of the toasted hazelnuts and the short texture are perfect to brighten up a cold, autumnal afternoon. They do come with a health warning though: it will be very hard to stop after just the one!

MAKES 20

100g (about ¾ cup) whole unblanched hazelnuts
200g (1½ cups) soft wheat 00 flour or plain (all-purpose) flour
130g (½ cup plus 1 tbsp) unsalted butter, softened and diced
100g (½ cup) caster (superfine) sugar
1 tsp vanilla bean paste
⅛ tsp salt
50g (1¾oz) egg (about 1 medium egg)
140g (½ cup) chocolate and hazelnut spread

1. Set the shelf in the middle of the oven and heat it to 180°C/350°F/ Gas mark 4. Put the hazelnuts on a baking tray and toast them for 10–12 minutes, shaking the tray midway to ensure an even baking. Allow the nuts to cool completely, then rub them between the palms of your hands to shed any loose flakes of skin. (If you are using pre-toasted hazelnuts, you can skip this step entirely.)

2. Put the hazelnuts and the flour in the bowl of a food processor and blitz at high speed just long enough to grind them to the texture of coarse sand. Set aside.

3. Put the butter, sugar, vanilla and salt in the bowl of a mixer with the paddle attachment and cream the mixture at medium-high speed until soft and homogeneous; it will take about 2 minutes. With the mixer still going, add the egg and mix until fully incorporated. Use a silicone spatula to scrape down the sides of the bowl if needed. Add the hazelnut and flour mixture and mix at low speed until it comes together as a soft dough. Wrap the dough in cling film and chill in the fridge for at least 30 minutes.

4. When ready to bake, set the shelf in the middle of the oven and preheat it to 180°C/350°F/Gas mark 4. Line two baking sheets with baking paper or silicone mats. Take the dough out of the fridge and divide it evenly into 20 lumps. Roll each one between the palms of your hands to shape them as small balls. Distribute them evenly on the two baking sheets. Make a dimple in the centre of each biscuit with the back of a teaspoon measuring spoon. Bake one tray at a time for 12–13 minutes or until the bottoms of the biscuits turn amber.

5. Leave the biscuits to cool for a few minutes on the trays, then transfer them to a wire rack to cool completely. Spoon ½ teaspoon of chocolate and hazelnut spread into the dimple of each biscuit. Nocciolatini keep for up to a week in an airtight container.

PREP TIME: 35 minutes, plus cooling and resting

TOTAL BAKING TIME: 24–26 minutes

BAKING TEMPERATURE: 180°C/350°F/Gas mark 4

BACI DI DAMA

Lady's kisses

Baci di dama are another delicious hazelnut-based creation of Piedmont, where these nuts grow in abundance and of unparalleled quality. The birthplace of the recipe is the city of Tortona, where these biscuits were invented almost two centuries ago. The name is a sensual reference to their typical shape, vaguely recalling a pair of pouting lips, about to kiss.

The recipe is very simple, and the best part is that it will fill your kitchen with the intoxicating scent of toasted hazelnuts, one of my most loved flavours in the baking world. Do not skip the resting times in the method as they are critical to produce biscuits of the right shape. The fiddliest part of the process is undoubtedly shaping the biscuits: to preserve their typical crunch, they have to be tiny. Each small ball of dough should be no bigger than one hazelnut in-shell. My technique will produce biscuits of the ideal size. You can make them bigger if you adjust the baking time accordingly, but the texture might suffer.

These dainty, elegant biscuits are unmistakably nutty, but if you prefer a more delicate taste, you can swap part or all of the hazelnuts for ground almonds. They are superb if paired with a cup of steaming hot chocolate and are perfect as a very thoughtful Valentine's gift.

MAKES 55

100g (¾ cup) whole blanched hazelnuts
100g (3½oz) caster (superfine) sugar
⅛ tsp salt
150g (1 cup plus 2 tbsp) soft wheat 00 flour or plain (all-purpose) flour
100g (scant ½ cup) cold unsalted butter, diced
20g (¾oz) egg white (about ½ medium egg white)
1 tsp vanilla bean paste
100g (3½oz) dark chocolate chips or a bar snapped into small pieces (70–75% cocoa solids)

1. Set the shelf in the middle of the oven and preheat it to 180°C/350°F/ Gas mark 4, unless your hazelnuts are pre-toasted, in which case you can skip this step. Scatter the hazelnuts on a baking tray and toast for 10–12 minutes, shaking the tray midway to ensure an even baking. Leave them to cool completely before moving to the next step.

2. Once cooled, put the hazelnuts, half the sugar and the salt in the bowl of a food processor and blitz at high speed just long enough to grind the mixture to the texture of fine sand. Use the pulse function, if available, and do not work it for any longer than strictly needed, or the hazelnuts will start leaching out oil, turning the sandy mixture into a pulp.

3. Transfer the mixture to a large bowl and add the flour, butter, egg white, vanilla and the remaining sugar. Work the mixture by pinching the pieces of butter with the tips of your fingers to break them into very small lumps. Keep working the mixture quickly without crushing it until it resembles fine, loose breadcrumbs.

4. Once all the butter has been completely incorporated, start crushing the mixture between your hands to form a stiff dough. Shape the dough roughly as a square, wrap it in cling film and chill for at least 1 hour.

5. When ready to shape the biscuits, line two baking sheets with baking paper or silicone mats. Prepare one extra sheet of baking paper on the worktop. Take the dough out of the fridge, place it over the sheet of baking paper and quickly roll it to 10mm (¼in) thickness, trying to keep the shape as square as possible.

Recipe continues overleaf

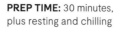

PREP TIME: 30 minutes, plus resting and chilling

TOTAL BAKING TIME: 22–24 minutes

BAKING TEMPERATURE: 180°C/350°F/Gas mark 4

6. Now cut the dough into little squares. The quickest way to do so is to slice it first horizontally into 2cm (¾in) wide strips using a knife or, better, a pastry cutter. Then cut the set of strips vertically into 2cm (¾in) wide squares. Each one will weigh about 4g (⅛oz). Roll each square of dough between your hands to form a small ball, place it on the baking sheet and gently press it with your thumb, just enough to stop it from rolling away. Repeat until all squares have been shaped, spreading the balls across the two trays, about 2.5cm (1in) apart. Place both trays in the freezer for about 1 hour, or until the dough is completely frozen.

7. When ready to bake, set the shelf in the middle of the oven and preheat it to 170°C/340°F/Gas mark 3½. Bake one tray at a time for about 11–12 minutes: baci di dama must go directly from freezer to oven, and they should be taken out while still pale; if the tops turn golden, they are overbaked. Check the bottoms as when they are golden, the biscuits are ready. Leave them to cool on the trays and only take them off the baking paper once completely cooled, or they will crumble.

8. Meanwhile, melt the chocolate by microwaving it at full power for 30 seconds. Stir well with a silicone spatula and, if bits of solid chocolate remain, give it subsequent 5-second bursts, stirring well between bursts, until all the chocolate is melted. Allow to rest at room temperature for a few minutes to stiffen up. To check whether it is ready, scoop a small amount with the spatula and let it fall back into the bowl: the chocolate is ready when it forms a blob that holds its shape without flowing back into the rest of the chocolate. While the chocolate stiffens up, arrange half the biscuits upside down on a wire rack.

9. Transfer the chocolate to a small piping bag with a 3–4mm (¼in) opening (no nozzle required) and pipe about ½ teaspoon of chocolate on each biscuit. You can also simply spoon dollops of chocolate onto the biscuits using 2 teaspoons, although the result might not be as neat. Pair each filled biscuit with its empty counterpart, slightly pressing them together, and place them back on the wire rack to set. Work quickly or the chocolate will set. Make sure the chocolate has hardened fully before taking the biscuits off the wire rack. They will keep for up to a week in an airtight container.

KRUMIRI

Krumiri were born at the end of the nineteenth century in Piedmont, with official documents placing their invention in 1878 in Casale Monferrato. Their handlebar shape reportedly honours the remarkable moustache of Vittorio Emanuele II, king of Italy, who died in that same year.

The original recipe is still a well-kept secret of the bakery that came up with it, but the simplicity of these biscuits has turned them into a national treasure, with versions close to the original found in pretty much every Italian family's recipe book.

The buttery, irresistible flavour of krumiri goes very well with hot drinks as well as sweet wines: they are perfect paired with a glass of sweet, red and sparkling Brachetto or dipped in either dark or milk chocolate sauce (pages 177 and 173).

The trickiest part is shaping these biscuits: krumiri are ideally piped with a cookie press as the dough is rather stiff and unwilling to pass through a star nozzle. However, my version is softened by a small addition of honey and milk, which makes it suitable for piping too. If you find the idea of squeezing hard on a piping bag too daunting, shape the dough using the method for the frollini di riso (page 94) instead.

MAKES 32

130g (½ cup plus 1 tbsp) unsalted butter, softened
140g (1 cup) icing (confectioner's) sugar
50g (1¾oz) egg yolk (about 3 medium egg yolks)
15g (1 tbsp) clear honey
1 tsp vanilla bean paste
350g (2⅔ cups) soft wheat 00 flour or plain (all-purpose) flour
⅛ tsp salt
50g (scant ¼ cup) whole milk

1. If the butter is at all cold or too stiff, soften it with a few 5-second bursts in the microwave, but let it rest for a couple of minutes between bursts to allow an even heat distribution. The butter should be soft and pliable, not melted.

2. Put the butter and icing sugar in the bowl of a stand mixer and cream with the paddle attachment until soft. Add the egg yolks, honey and vanilla, then run the mixer at high speed until the mixture is pale and fluffy; it will take a couple of minutes. Scrape down the sides of the bowl with a silicone spatula at least once during the process.

3. Sift the flour into the mixer bowl, add the salt and milk, then run the mixer at its lowest speed until the dough comes together. Turn out the dough onto a clean and dry worktop; you might need a curved-edge plastic scraper to collect all the dough in the bottom of the bowl. Pat the dough down with the palm of your hand and, using a straight-edge scraper, lift one side and fold it over. Repeat the patting and folding a few times until the dough is smooth. Wrap in cling film and set it aside to rest at room temperature for at least 1 hour. Do not put it in the fridge or it will become too stiff to be piped.

4. When ready to shape the krumiri, set the shelf in the middle of the oven and preheat it to 180°C/350°F/Gas mark 4. Line two baking sheets with baking paper or silicone mats. If you are using paper, smear the sheets with a dab of butter to secure the paper in place.

Recipe continues overleaf

PREP TIME: 20 minutes, plus resting time

TOTAL BAKING TIME: 24–28 minutes

BAKING TEMPERATURE: 180°C/350°F/Gas mark 4

nut-free

5. Place a small amount of dough in the piping bag with a 15mm (⅝in) star nozzle or, if you have one, in a cookie press. Piping a small amount of dough at a time will make the task easier. Pipe the biscuits directly on the lined baking sheet, as 7–8cm (3-in) long, handlebar-shaped noodles. You should be able to accommodate up to 16 biscuits on a standard size baking sheet.

6. Bake the krumiri, one tray at a time, for 12–14 minutes, and check the bottoms of the biscuits rather than the tops: when their bottoms are golden, they are ready. Leave them to cool completely before taking them off the baking paper and serve at room temperature. They keep for up to a week in an airtight container.

BISCOTTI NOCI E MARMELLATA

Jammy walnuts

The inclusion of ground walnuts in the dough means these biscuits are unusually short and crumbly as well as extremely flavoursome. The combination of warm spices, slightly bitter nuts and sugary jam makes them an ideal wintry treat – perfect with a coffee or afternoon tea.

I have paired my biscotti with apricot, but any jam you have in your cupboard would do. However, the best match for the nutty and cinnamon flavour of these biscuits is an apple compote: you can make one following the recipe for the filling of my gobeletti (page 74).

The dough for biscotti noci e marmellata is particularly easy to make: it literally takes less than 5 minutes and it is all done in the food processor, meaning minimal washing-up too.

MAKES 9

220g (1⅔ cups) soft wheat 00 flour or plain (all-purpose) flour
90g (scant ½ cup) unsalted butter, cold
60g (⅓ cup) dark soft brown sugar
60g (about ¾ cup) walnut pieces
½ tsp baking powder
¾ tsp ground cinnamon
50g (1¾oz) egg (about 1 medium egg), cold
1 tsp vanilla bean paste
120g (4¼oz) apricot jam (preserve)
icing (confectioner's) sugar, for dusting

1. Put the flour, butter, sugar, walnuts, baking powder and cinnamon in the bowl of a food processor and blitz for about 1 minute, until the mixture has the texture of fine sand. Add the egg and vanilla and blitz again to form a dough. Turn it out onto a clean and dry worktop, pat it down with the palm of your hand then, using a straight-edge scraper, lift one side and fold it over. Repeat the patting and folding a few times until the mixture looks smooth. Shape the dough as a 2-cm (¾-in) thick disc, wrap in cling film and chill it in the fridge for at least 30 minutes.
2. When ready to shape the biscuits, set the shelf in the middle of the oven and preheat it to 180°C/350°F/Gas mark 4. Line two baking sheets with baking paper or silicone mats.
3. Place the dough between two large sheets of baking paper and roll it out to 5mm (¼in) thickness: the dough is quite crumbly so handle it gently. Cut the biscuit shapes with a 7cm (2¾in) pastry cutter. Re-roll the offcuts until you have 18 biscuits. Transfer the biscuits to the lined baking sheets and cut 3cm (1¼in) holes in half of them. Bake one sheet at a time for 12–13 minutes or until the dough looks slightly puffed and its surface is dull. Leave the biscuits to cool on the sheet for a few minutes and, when cool enough to touch, transfer to a wire rack to cool completely.
4. Meanwhile heat the jam in the microwave for about 60–70 seconds. Stir it well and leave it to cool slightly, then spoon a heaped teaspoonful into the centre of each biscuit without a hole and pair it with the holed counterpart. You can spoon extra jam in the holes if you like them jammier. Dust lightly with icing sugar and transfer to a serving tray. Biscotti noci e marmellata keep for up to a week in an airtight container.

SETTEMBRINI

Fig rolls

Mulino Bianco, a leading Italian brand of baked goods, used the name settembrini to launch its fig rolls on the market in the early eighties. The name is a clear reference to the month of September, when figs are abundant in the Italian countryside, and the timing is perfect to bake a batch of these sweet and flavoursome biscuits. The shell is made of pasta frolla, the typical Italian shortcrust pastry, while the filling is a simple mixture of fig jam, almonds and walnuts. The preparation is easy and straightforward as the pastry can be prepared up to a couple of days in advance and stored in the fridge; the shaping is similar to mostaccioli, so you can refer to the step-by-step photos and video on (page 139) for guidance.

MAKES 12

For the pastry

100g (scant ½ cup) unsalted butter, at room temperature

100g (½ cup) caster (superfine) sugar

50g (1¾oz) egg (about 1 medium egg), at room temperature

1 tsp vanilla bean paste

⅛ tsp salt

zest of ½ unwaxed organic lemon

200g (1½ cups) soft wheat 00 flour or plain (all-purpose) flour, plus extra for dusting

50g (generous ⅓ cup) wholemeal (whole wheat) flour

½ tsp ground cinnamon

For the filling and assembly

210g (7oz) fig jam (preserve)

30g (about ⅓ cup) walnut pieces, roughly chopped to the size of peas

20g (3 tbsp) ground almonds

1 tsp vanilla bean paste

zest of ½ unwaxed organic lemon

1 egg yolk

1 tbsp whole milk

1. Put the butter, sugar, egg, vanilla, salt and lemon zest in the bowl of a food processor and blitz until fully combined as a smooth cream. Transfer the mixture to a large bowl and add the flours and cinnamon. Combine by hand until the pastry comes together in a soft and smooth dough. Wrap it in cling film and chill in the fridge for at least 30 minutes.

2. For the filling, put the jam in a microwave-safe bowl large enough to accommodate all the ingredients and microwave it just long enough to soften it, about 40 seconds. Add the walnuts, almonds, vanilla and lemon zest to the jam and mix well to combine. Cover with a plate and chill in the fridge for at least 15 minutes.

3. Prepare an egg wash by beating the yolk and milk in a small cup. Line one baking sheet with baking paper. Take the pastry out of the fridge and divide it into two halves. Set half aside and roll the other half to 5mm (¼in) thickness on a lightly floured, 35-cm (14-in) long sheet of baking paper. Shape the pastry as a rectangle, about 15 x 25cm (6 x 10in), and position it on the worktop with a long side facing you. Spoon half the filling onto the middle third of the sheet of pastry, distributing it evenly over its whole length: leave the top and bottom thirds of the pastry free of filling. Fold the bottom third over the filling, then brush the edge of the flap with egg wash. Fold the top third over the filling so that it overlaps the egg-washed edge by about 1cm (½in) and press very gently to seal.

4. Using the baking paper under the pastry, flip the whole log over so that the seal is on the underside. Brush the top with more egg wash, trim the two short edges, then slice the log into 6 equal pieces. Arrange them on the baking tray, and put them in the fridge while you repeat the process with the remaining half of the pastry and filling.

5. When ready to bake, set the shelf in the middle of the oven and preheat it to 180°C/350°F/Gas mark 4. Bake the rolls for 22–23 minutes, then leave them to cool slightly on the baking sheet before transferring them to a wire rack to cool completely. Settembrini are best eaten within a day of baking as they tend to soften over time, but they will keep for up to 3 days under a cake dome.

PREP TIME: 25 minutes, plus resting and chilling

TOTAL BAKING TIME: 22–23 minutes

BAKING TEMPERATURE: 180°C/350°F/Gas mark 4

PIZZICOTTI AL MANDARINO

Clementine and almond cookies

Pizzicotti literally means 'little pinches' and it refers to the three-scallop shape given to the biscuits by pinching the dough when forming them. Like many almond-based recipes, pizzicotti are originally from southern Italy and are particularly common in Sicily. However, given their snow-white coating, they have become a very common sight in the Christmas period all over the country.

The sweetness of pizzicotti makes them an excellent complement to an espresso at the end of an indulgent lunch and, although one of these accompanies very well a mid-morning tea, it is absolutely glorious when served next to a steaming cup of hot chocolate.

The dough can be prepared up to a couple of days in advance and stored in the fridge wrapped in cling film, ready to be shaped and baked at your convenience.

MAKES 28

peel of 1 unwaxed organic clementine, washed and dried
250g (2½ cups) ground almonds
200g (generous 1 cup) caster (superfine) sugar
⅛ tsp salt
60g (2¼oz) egg white (about 2 medium egg whites)
1 tsp natural almond extract
2 tsp clear honey
about 40g (⅓ cup) icing (confectioner's) sugar, for coating, plus extra for dusting

1. Chop the clementine peel very finely and add it to the bowl of a food processor with the ground almonds, sugar and salt. Blitz for a few seconds just to combine. Add the egg white, almond extract and honey and blitz again until the mixture forms a stiff paste. Turn out the paste onto a clean dry worktop, pat it down with the palm of your hand then, using a straight-edge scraper, lift one side and fold it over. Repeat the patting and folding a few times until the mixture looks smooth. Wrap the dough in cling film and chill it in the fridge for at least 1 hour.

2. When ready to shape the pizzicotti, set the shelf in the middle of the oven and preheat it to 180°C/350°F/Gas mark 4. Line two baking sheets with baking paper or silicone mats.

3. Dust the worktop generously with icing sugar and have ready more icing sugar on a plate for later. Take the dough out of the fridge and roll it over the sugared worktop to shape it into a large sausage, about 3cm (1¼in) thick. Chop your sausage into 28 small lumps; they will be about 20g (¾oz) each – while there is no need to weigh them individually, equal-sized lumps will guarantee an even bake.

4. Roll each lump of dough between the palms of your hands to shape it as a little ball, then drop it into the icing sugar on the plate. Roll each ball of dough several times in the icing sugar until it is fully coated and looks stark white.

5. Divide the pizzicotti between the baking sheets and, when placing them, gently pinch each ball using your thumb, index and middle fingers to give the characteristic scalloped shape.

6. Bake one tray at a time, for 12–14 minutes, until a few golden cracks appear on their sugared surface. Let them cool completely before taking them off the baking paper and serve at room temperature. They keep for up to 2 weeks in an airtight container.

gluten-free, dairy-free **PREP TIME:** 20 minutes, plus resting time **TOTAL BAKING TIME:** 24–28 minutes **BAKING TEMPERATURE:** 180°C/350°F/Gas mark 4

NIDI DI COCCO ALL'ALBICOCCA

Apricot macaroons

Macaroons were always included in the Christmas biscuit selection that my family used to give to family and friends. Their snow-white appearance and flaky texture make them a perfect complement for a festive platter. I have tested several recipes over the years, but I must admit that none beats the one my dad has been using for decades: his secret was to soak the desiccated coconut in hot sugar syrup before folding in the meringue, softening the flakes and adding moisture to the mix, to deliver macaroons that are always crispy on the outside, while retaining a soft and chewy core.

I like to shape my macaroons as rather substantial nidi – nests – filled with a dollop of apricot jam: I find that the tartness of the apricots cuts through and balances out the sweetness of the coconut particularly well. However, you can swap the jam for hazelnut spread, if you are after a more indulgent treat, or omit it altogether and have the macaroon either plain or drizzled with streaks of dark chocolate.

MAKES 20

250g (2¾ cups) unsweetened desiccated (shredded) coconut
80g (scant ⅓ cup) water
80g (scant ½ cup) caster (superfine) sugar
70g (2½oz) egg white (about 2 medium egg whites)
⅛ tsp salt
100g (scant 1 cup) icing (confectioner's) sugar
1 tsp vanilla bean paste
½ tsp natural almond extract
130g (4½oz) apricot jam (preserve)

1. Put the coconut in a heatproof bowl and set aside. Add the water and caster sugar (in this order) to a small saucepan and bring to a simmer over a medium heat; keep simmering the solution for 2 minutes to make a light syrup, then, while it is still hot, pour it over the coconut. Mix well to moisten the coconut fully, then leave to cool.

2. Add the egg white and salt to a clean metal, ceramic or glass bowl and whisk at medium speed with a handheld electric whisk or a stand mixer until the whisks leave visible marks on the egg white surface; it will take about 1 minute. Add the icing sugar, a tablespoon at a time, and keep whisking to make a stiff meringue; it will take about 2 minutes. Spoon the meringue into the coconut, add the vanilla and almond extract, then gently fold into the mixture until fully combined.

3. Line a baking sheet with baking paper or a silicone mat. Set the shelf in the middle of the oven and preheat it to 160°C/320°F/Gas mark 3.

4. Meanwhile, divide the mixture into 20 dollops, each roughly the size of a plum. Shape each dollop into a rough ball using 2 tablespoons (or your hands, if you find it easier) before dropping them onto the baking sheet. Using wet fingers, pat down each dollop to shape it as a 6–7-cm (2½-in) diameter disc, about 2cm (¾in) high, then create a dimple in each with your index finger: this is where the jam will go.

5. Bake the macaroons for 27–29 minutes until the edges and tops just start to turn golden, then leave them to cool down completely before taking them off the baking paper.

6. Spoon about 1 teaspoon of apricot jam onto each macaroon and serve at room temperature; they keep for up to a week in an airtight container.

PREP TIME: 20 minutes　　**TOTAL BAKING TIME:** 27–29 minutes　　**BAKING TEMPERATURE:** 160°C/320°F/Gas mark 3　　gluten-free, dairy-free

LINGUE DI GATTO

Cat's tongues

Despite the uninviting name, deriving from their resemblance to a feline tongue, lingue di gatto rank very high on my list of favourite biscuits. Their intensely buttery flavour and crispy, chewy texture make these wafer-thin delicacies an irresistible treat for kids and grown-ups alike.

The first evidence of written recipes dates back to the early twentieth century but some historians place it way back in the seventeenth century. Today, variations are common across Europe, where they have become a staple alongside ice creams, an elegant decoration for cakes and an indulgent accompaniment to sweet wines. Personally, I love them on their own or dipped in either my milk chocolate (page 173) or coffee sauce (page 180).

As if their deliciousness was not enough, these biscuits are deceptively easy to make: the batter is literally ready in 5 minutes and, if you do not like piping, you can simply spoon it on the baking tray. Combine the ingredients very gently, and avoid incorporating any air, as this provides a biscuit with a more pleasant bite. The final step involving a rolling pin is not strictly necessary, but the curved shape undeniably adds an element of effortless sophistication, so... why not?

MAKES 24

50g (3½ tbsp) unsalted butter, softened
50g (about ⅓ cup) icing (confectioner's) sugar
50g (1¾oz) egg white (less than 2 medium egg whites), at room temperature
50g (6 tbsp) plain (all-purpose) flour
1 tsp vanilla bean paste
⅛ tsp salt

1. Set the shelf in the middle of the oven and preheat it to 180°C/350°F/Gas mark 4. Line two baking sheets with baking paper or silicone mats.
2. Put the butter in a medium bowl and cream it lightly with a silicone spatula until it has the consistency of thick custard. If the butter is too stiff to cream, give it a few 5-second bursts in the microwave, mixing it well between subsequent bursts.
3. Add the icing sugar to the bowl and, using the spatula, incorporate it into the butter. Add the egg white, flour, vanilla and salt, and keep mixing until the ingredients come together as a smooth and homogenous paste.
4. Secure the baking paper to the baking sheets with a smear of the batter. Spoon dollops of batter, roughly ½ tablespoon each, onto the lined sheets, keeping them at least 6cm (2½in) apart, as the batter will spread significantly. For longer, finger-like biscuits, pipe the batter into 8-cm (3¼-in) long noodles with an 8mm (⅜in) plain nozzle. Bake one tray at a time for 12–13 minutes or until the edges of the biscuits turn a deep caramel colour.
5. As soon as the biscuits come out of the oven, use a spatula or a knife to lift them gently and lay them on a rolling pin. Leave them there to cool completely and set. Lingue di gatto keep for up to 2 weeks in an airtight container and can be frozen for up to a month.

PREP TIME: less than 10 minutes

TOTAL BAKING TIME: 24–26 minutes

BAKING TEMPERATURE: 180°C/350°F/Gas mark 4

nut-free

PASTICCINI AL CAFFÈ
Coffee nuts

Pasticcini al caffè are one of the many variants of the popular marzipan cookies common all over Italy, especially in the central and southern regions. This combination delivers a cookie with a powerful, complex, almost adult taste, where the slight bitterness of coffee and walnut balances out the sweetness of the marzipan extremely well.

My recipe works with either wheat- or corn-based flour, so for a gluten-free version you can use cornflour without sacrificing the taste or the texture of the cookie. If you have instant coffee granules, I recommend grinding them first into a fine powder with a pestle and mortar as it will incorporate much better into the dough. They are delicious on their own and are the perfect addition to a tray of mixed cookies, like apricot macaroons (page 120) or pizzicotti al mandarino (page 122).

MAKES about 16

200g (2 cups) ground almonds
180g (1½ cups) icing (confectioner's) sugar
⅛ tsp salt
60g (2½oz) egg white (about 2 medium egg whites)
1 tsp natural almond extract
30g (¼ cup) cornflour (cornstarch) or plain (all-purpose) flour
1½ tbsp unsweetened cocoa powder
1½ tbsp instant coffee powder or granules
about 50g (¼ cup) demerara (light brown) sugar
16 walnut halves

1. Put the ground almonds, icing sugar and salt in the bowl of a food processor and blitz for a few seconds to combine the powders. Add the egg white and almond extract then blitz again until the mixture forms a thick paste. Sift in the flour and cocoa powder then add the coffee powder. Blitz again until the mixture comes together as a stiff dough.

2. Turn out the dough onto a clean dry worktop; at this stage it will be very sticky and it will not be fully combined yet: you might still see streaks of light and dark dough. Pat it down with the palm of your hand then, using a straight-edge scraper, lift one side and fold it over. Repeat the patting and folding a few times until the mixture looks smooth and without streaks. Wrap the dough in cling film and chill for at least 30 minutes.

3. Meanwhile, set the shelf in the middle of the oven and preheat it to 150°C/300°F/Gas mark 2. Line a large baking sheet with baking paper or a silicone mat.

4. Take the dough out of the fridge; it will look much drier now and it will be much easier to handle. Quickly roll it on a clean and dry worktop to shape it into a long sausage, about 3cm (1¼in) thick. Chop it into 16 cylinder-shaped lumps, each about 30g (1oz) – while there is no need to weigh them individually, equal-sized biscuits will guarantee an even bake.

5. Put the demerara sugar in a small bowl and set aside. Take one lump of dough and pat it between your hands to shape as an oval, about 2cm (¾in) thick, so that it resembles a large coffee bean. If the dough is too sticky, moisten your hands with no more than a drop of water. Place one half-walnut on the top face of the cookie and secure it by pushing it gently into the dough, then dip it into the demerara sugar to coat it lightly. Repeat the process with all the other pieces of dough and progressively arrange your coffee nuts on the baking sheet. Bake them for 25–27 minutes until a few cracks start to appear on the surface. Leave them to cool completely before taking them off the baking paper and serve at room temperature. They keep for up to 2 weeks in an airtight container.

gluten-free, dairy-free

PREP TIME: less than 20 minutes, plus resting time

TOTAL BAKING TIME: 25–27 minutes

BAKING TEMPERATURE: 150°C/300°F/Gas mark 2

Amarena cherry rolls

Walking into any pasticceria, bakery or coffee shop in Naples, you are guaranteed to find generous arrays of biscotti all'amarena lining the shop windows. Local pastry chefs created them to upcycle leftovers no longer suitable for sale: cake sponge, croissants and biscuits would be crushed, mixed with generous handfuls of amarena cherries in syrup (page 19), and wrapped in a crumbly layer of shortcrust pastry. My version uses a filling based on dry sweet biscuits, but you can certainly go back to the origins and fill them with leftover panettone, stale biscuits or unused cake. These biscuits are assembled and shaped in the same way as mostaccioli, so refer to the step-by-step photos on page 138 for guidance.

MAKES 12

For the pastry
100g (scant ½ cup) unsalted butter, at room temperature, plus extra for greasing
100g (½ cup) caster (superfine) sugar
50g (1¾oz) egg (about 1 medium egg), at room temperature
1 tsp vanilla bean paste
zest of 1 unwaxed organic lemon
⅛ tsp salt
250g (1¾ cups plus 2 tbsp) soft wheat 00 flour or plain (all-purpose) flour, plus extra for dusting
icing (confectioner's) sugar, for dusting

For the filling and assembly
250g (9oz) Rich Tea biscuits or other light, crisp sweet variety
250g (9oz) Amarena cherries in syrup (drained weight)
60g (4 tbsp) syrup from the Amarena cherries, plus 1 tbsp for coating
20g (4 tsp) rum
1 tsp vanilla bean paste
1 egg yolk

1. Put the butter, sugar, egg, vanilla, lemon zest and salt in the bowl of a food processor and blitz until fully combined as a homogeneous cream. Transfer the mixture to a large bowl and add the flour. Combine by hand until the pastry comes together as a soft and smooth dough. Wrap in cling film and chill it in the fridge for at least 30 minutes.

2. Meanwhile, make the filling. Put the biscuits in the bowl of a food processor and blitz until they resemble fine sand. (Alternatively, you can bash them in a double-wrapped food bag with a rolling pin.) Put the drained Amarena cherries in a bowl large enough to accommodate all the ingredients and roughly mash them with a fork. Add the syrup, rum, vanilla and crushed biscuits to the bowl. Mix by hand or with a spoon until the filling comes together as a stiff and sticky mixture. Lay a 50-cm (20-in) long sheet of cling film on the worktop, then tip the filling onto it. Wrap the filling in the cling film and shape it as 40-cm (16-in) long log, twist the ends and chill in the freezer for at least 15 minutes.

3. When ready to bake, set the shelf in the middle of the oven and preheat it to 200°C/400°F/Gas mark 6. Line a baking sheet with baking paper or a silicone mat. Prepare an egg wash by beating the egg yolk with 1 tablespoon of cherry syrup. Set aside for later.

4. Roll the chilled pastry to 5mm (¼in) thickness over a lightly floured, 45-cm (18-in) long sheet of baking paper. Shape the pastry as a rectangle, about 15 x 40cm (6 x 16in), with a longer side facing you. Brush the surface of the pastry sheet with some of the egg wash, then place the chilled filling on the pastry. Use the baking paper to lift the pastry and wrap it around the filling, slightly overlapping the join; press gently on the overlap to seal it.

5. Using the baking paper, flip the whole log over so that the seal is on the underside. Flatten gently with the palm of your hand to about a 3cm (1¼in) thickness. Brush the top with the remaining egg wash, then decorate it by drawing wavy lines with the tines of a fork held face down. Trim the ends with a sharp knife, then slice it into 12 equal pieces, about 3cm (1¼in) wide. Arrange them on the baking sheet and bake for 15–16 minutes or until the top is browned. Leave them to cool slightly on the sheet before transferring them to a wire rack to cool completely. They keep for up to a week in an airtight container.

PREP TIME: 30 minutes, plus resting and chilling

TOTAL BAKING TIME: 15–16 minutes

BAKING TEMPERATURE: 200°C/400°F/Gas mark 6

nut-free

SUSAMELLI

Honey cookies

Susamelli are fatless cookies typically baked in the Christmas period, particularly in the areas around Naples. Despite being made with lots of honey, they are delicately flavoured and not overly sweet. The texture of susamelli is satisfyingly chewy, but they must not be overbaked or they will turn quite hard rather quickly.

The recipe dates back to the eighteenth century at least; apparently, the name originates from the sesame seeds used to coat early versions of this cookie. These days, susamelli tend to be decorated with almonds, and they are always formed in the traditional S-shape.

Given their texture, the best way to savour these cookies is dipped in a drink: susamelli go particularly well with a good glass of mulled wine or chilled spumante, although they are a perfect companion for a cup of strong coffee or tea.

MAKES 16

80g (about ⅔ cup) whole blanched almonds, plus 48 extra, to decorate
80g (scant ½ cup) caster (superfine) sugar
250g (1¾ cups plus 2 tbsp) soft wheat 00 flour or plain (all-purpose) flour, plus extra for dusting
½ tbsp pisto (page 21) (alternatively, use 1 tsp ground cinnamon, ¼ tsp ground cloves, ⅛ tsp ground black pepper and ⅛ tsp ground nutmeg)
½ tsp baking ammonia* or bicarbonate of soda (baking soda)
250g (1 cup) clear honey
1 tsp vanilla bean paste

1. Set the shelf in the middle of the oven and preheat it to 180°C/350°F/ Gas mark 4. Line two baking trays with baking paper or silicone mats.
2. Put the almonds and half the sugar in the bowl of a food processor. Blitz at high speed until the mixture has the texture of coarse sand. Transfer the mixture to a medium bowl and add the flour, pisto and baking ammonia. Mix well with a spoon until fully combined.
3. Pour the honey into a small saucepan and add the remaining sugar. Warm over a low heat while stirring continuously, until the sugar has completely dissolved. Remove from the heat just before it starts simmering.
4. Make a well in the middle of the dry ingredients and pour in the hot honey, then add the vanilla. Mix with a spoon and, when the dough starts coming together, turn it onto a clean and dry worktop. At this stage the dough should be cool enough to handle with your bare hands, so knead it by hand until homogeneous. The dough will be rather sticky, so a straight-edge scraper will be essential to lift it off the worktop.
5. Dust the worktop and the dough with flour and use the scraper to divide the dough into 16, roughly equal, lumps. Roll them into sticks 10–12cm (roughly 4in) long, then give them an 'S' shape and arrange them on the baking trays, keeping them at least 5cm (2in) apart as they will spread significantly while baking.
6. Decorate the top of each cookie with three whole almonds. Bake them, one tray at a time, for no longer than 11–12 minutes; the cookies will be very soft when they come out of the oven, so wait until they are fully cooled before taking them off the baking paper. Susamelli keep for up to 2 weeks in an airtight container but, given the high honey content, they are very sensitive to moisture and will soften over time.

*Also known as baker's ammonia or ammonium carbonate, this is sourced through online retailers, especially from Italian or German vendors, as ammoniaca per dolci or Hirschhornsalz, respectively.

egg-free, dairy-free **PREP TIME:** 15 minutes **TOTAL BAKING TIME:** 22–24 minutes **BAKING TEMPERATURE:** 180°C/350°F/Gas mark 4

PASTICCINI DI FROLLA MONTATA
<u>Butter biscuits</u>

Frolla montata is one of the pillars of Italian baking. It shares its name and ingredients with pasta frolla, the quintessential Italian shortcrust pastry used in a vast number of bakes, but the preparation method is different: frolla montata must be whipped vigorously and long enough to incorporate lots of air into the pastry. This, together with the relatively high butter content, will create pasticcini (meaning little pastries) with the crumbliest and shortest texture.

The warm, sweet vanilla and butter flavour of the base pastry makes it a perfect canvas for whatever coating, topping or decoration you wish to use. You can prepare a chocolate version too (see photo on page 134) by swapping 3 tablespoons of flour with the same amount of unsweetened cocoa powder.

This dough requires no resting, so it can be piped immediately, but I recommend freezing the shaped biscuits before baking so their features remain sharp. If you have never used a piping bag, this is a safe way to start because any misshapen biscuit can be thrown back into the bag and re-piped. The dough is rather stiff, ideal for a cookie press or a canvas or nylon piping bag. If using disposable bags, it is best to use two, one inside the other, and to avoid overfilling it with dough.

MAKES 22–28

150g (⅔ cup) unsalted butter, softened and diced
100g (generous ¾ cup) icing (confectioner's) sugar
2 tsp vanilla bean paste
⅛ tsp salt
50g (1¾oz) egg (about 1 medium egg), at room temperature
210g (generous 1½ cups) soft wheat 00 flour or plain (all-purpose) flour

For the decoration (optional)
glacé (candied) cherries (halved) or whole hazelnuts
75g (½ cup) chopped unsalted pistachio kernels
100g (3½oz) dark, ruby or white chocolate (chips, or bar broken into small pieces)
peach or apricot jam (preserve)

1. If the butter is at all cold or stiff, soften it with a few 5-second bursts in the microwave, but let it rest for a couple of minutes between bursts to allow an even heat distribution. The butter should be soft and pliable, not melted. Line two baking trays with baking paper.

2. Put the softened butter, icing sugar, vanilla and salt in a bowl large enough to accommodate all the ingredients. Whisk the mixture at high speed with a handheld electric whisk (or use a stand mixer) until pale and fluffy; it will take at least 5 minutes. Use a silicone spatula to scrape down the sides of the bowl at least once midway through the process.

3. Beat the egg and, with the whisk still going, trickle it slowly into the butter mixture, and whisk for a further minute to incorporate it fully. Scrape the sides of the bowl again, if necessary. The mixture will become fluffier and more aerated. Sift the flour into the bowl and mix at the lowest speed until homogeneous.

4. Transfer the mixture to a piping bag with a star nozzle: I use a 12mm (½in) open star nozzle for U-shapes and swirls, a 15mm (⅝in) open star one for star shapes and a 12mm (½in) fine star one for logs. Secure the baking paper to the trays with four little smudges of pastry under the corners, then pipe the mixture into straight logs, U-shapes, swirls or stars. Decorate the star-shaped biscuits with hazelnuts or halved glacé cherries, then chill them all in the freezer for at least 20 minutes. Meanwhile, set the shelf just above the middle of the oven and preheat it to 200°C/400°F/Gas mark 6.

PREP TIME: 40 minutes, plus chilling time

BAKING TIME: 18–24 minutes, depending on size

BAKING TEMPERATURE: 200°C/400°F/Gas mark 6

5. Bake the biscuits straight from the freezer, one tray at a time, for about 10 minutes: smaller shapes may only need 9 minutes while larger ones may need up to 12 minutes. The biscuits are done when the edges start to turn golden. Leave them to cool for a couple of minutes, then transfer them to a wire rack to cool completely. Keep the baking paper for the decorating step.

6. If decorating, put the chocolate in a small bowl and microwave it for 1 minute, then stir well. Keep microwaving it in 10-second bursts, stirring well between subsequent bursts until completely melted. Set aside to cool for a few minutes. Put the chopped pistachios in another small bowl.

7. Holding the U-shaped biscuits by the bend, dip the two ends into the chocolate then place them on the baking paper to set. Dip the log-shaped ones into the chocolate too, coating about a third of each biscuit, then dip them in the chopped nuts before leaving them on the baking paper to set. Warm about 10g (¼oz) of jam per swirl-shaped biscuit in the microwave, stir well and drop 1 heaped teaspoonful into the centre of each swirl. Pasticcini keep for up to 3 days in an airtight container.

ROCCOCÒ

Roccocò are rustic, dry biscuits traditionally baked in Campania in the Christmas period. The combination of toasted almonds, citrus peel and pisto (page 21) makes them truly aromatic. In my family home, the scent of roccocò is undeniably what Christmas smells like. The original recipe is very old (dating back to the fourteenth century) and completely fatless; in fact, it makes rather hard biscuits. However, my family recipe includes honey and a dash of vegetable oil to produce a softer crumb. Although the resulting texture is pleasantly crisp, roccocò are still better served with or dipped in sweet wine. In principle, they are intended for the end of a celebratory meal, but they are an unmissable festive treat when dipped in caffè latte for breakfast! The recipe calls for baking ammonia (see footnote opposite) as a leavening agent and the extra crispness this delivers is definitely worth the extra effort required to source it. Bicarbonate of soda can be used instead, although the biscuits will have a slightly harder bite. For an egg-free version, omit the final brushing with egg yolk.

MAKES 16

130g (1 cup) whole unblanched almonds, plus 48 extra, to decorate
peel of 1 unwaxed organic clementine, washed and dried
250g (1¾ cups plus 2 tbsp) soft wheat 00 flour or plain (all-purpose) flour, plus extra for dusting
170g (generous ¾ cup) caster (superfine) sugar
zest of 1 unwaxed organic orange
½ tbsp pisto (page 21) (alternatively, use 1 tsp ground cinnamon, ¼ tsp ground cloves, ⅛ tsp ground black pepper and ⅛ tsp ground nutmeg)
½ tbsp unsweetened cocoa powder
¼ tsp salt
½ tsp baking ammonia* or bicarbonate of soda (baking soda)
50g (3 tbsp) clear honey
50g (3 tbsp plus 1 tsp) water
30g (3 tbsp) vegetable oil (preferably corn or sunflower)
1 tsp vanilla bean paste
1 egg yolk, beaten, for brushing (avoid for an egg-free version)

1. Set the shelf in the middle of the oven and preheat it to 180°C/350°F/Gas mark 4. If your almonds are pre-toasted, you can skip the rest of this step. Scatter the 130g (1 cup) of almonds over a baking tray and, once the oven is at temperature, toast them for 10–12 minutes, shaking the tray midway to ensure an even baking. When they are done, take the almonds out of the oven and leave them to cool completely before moving to the next step. Leave the oven on.

2. Meanwhile, line two baking trays with baking paper or silicone mats. Finely chop the clementine peel and place it in a bowl, large enough to accommodate all the ingredients. Once cooled, coarsely chop the toasted almonds by hand with a sharp knife and add them to the same bowl: roccocò are rather rustic, so pea-sized pieces are perfectly acceptable, there is no need to go very fine.

3. Add the flour, sugar, orange zest, pisto, cocoa, salt and baking ammonia to the bowl, and mix with a spoon until fully combined. Make a well in the centre of the dry ingredients, then add the honey, water, oil and vanilla, and incorporate them into the dry ingredients by hand. The mixture will feel dry to start with, but it will come together as you keep kneading it. Turn out onto a floured worktop and keep working it by hand until it comes together as a stiff, slightly sticky dough.

4. Lightly dust the worktop with flour and divide the dough into 16 equal pieces: they will be about 40g (1½oz) each. Roll each piece into a 20cm (8in) noodle, always keeping the worktop well-floured. Form each noodle into a ring about 8cm (3in) in diameter and place them on the prepared baking trays, eight biscuits per tray. Gently flatten the dough, only a little, with wet fingers.

5. Rinse the extra 48 almonds under running water and place three, still wet, on each biscuit. Generously brush the tops with beaten egg yolk. Bake them, one tray at a time, for 15–17 minutes. The biscuits will be rather

---

 egg-free, dairy-free **PREP TIME:** 30 minutes **BAKING TIME:** 30–34 minutes **BAKING TEMPERATURE:** 180°C/350°F/Gas mark 4

soft when they come out of the oven, so allow them to cool completely before peeling off the baking paper. Roccocò are very sensitive to moisture and will soften over time, but they will keep for up to 2 weeks in an airtight container.

*Also known as baker's ammonia or ammonium carbonate, this is sourced through online retailers, especially from Italian or German vendors, as ammoniaca per dolci or Hirschhornsalz, respectively.

Several (and often different) sweet treats are called mostaccioli in Italy: the name probably comes from mosto or 'must', unfermented fresh grape juice, often used as a sweetener before sugar became an affordable commodity. Nowadays a staple on the Christmas table, their origin is lost in the mists of time, with references dating back to the sixteenth century. My version is richly spiced, coated in dark chocolate and filled with a fragrant nut and fruit mixture. The latter is traditionally made with quince paste, loosened with rum, but you can replace it with apricot jam: in this case reduce the rum to just 15g (1 tbsp) and use 90g (3¼oz) of crushed biscuits to keep the texture at the right level of softness. The mostaccioli filling is also ideal to use up old cake, stale croissants or leftover panettone as alternatives to biscuits. For a vegan version, replace the honey with agave or golden syrup.

MAKES 12

For the dough
230g (1¾ cups) soft wheat 00 flour or plain (all-purpose) flour, plus extra for dusting
70g (⅓ cup) caster (superfine) sugar
20g (generous 2 tbsp) unsweetened cocoa powder
½ tbsp pisto (page 21) (or 1 tsp ground cinnamon, ¼ tsp ground cloves, ⅛ tsp ground black pepper and ⅛ tsp ground nutmeg)
½ tsp bicarbonate of soda (baking soda)
zest of 1 unwaxed organic orange
130g (scant ½ cup) clear honey
30g (2 tbsp) water
1 tsp vanilla bean paste

For the filling
60g (2¼oz) Rich Tea biscuits or other light, crisp sweet variety
1 tbsp unsweetened cocoa powder
50g (about 2½ cups) mixed candied peel, diced
50g (scant ½ cup) raisins
30g (¼ cup) toasted chopped hazelnuts
1 tsp vanilla bean paste
200g (7oz) quince paste
30g (2 tbsp) dark rum or Strega

1. Put the flour, sugar, cocoa, pisto, bicarbonate of soda and orange zest in a bowl large enough to accommodate all the ingredients and mix until fully combined. Warm the honey in the microwave for about 20 seconds. Add the honey to the dry ingredients, along with the water and the vanilla. Mix with a spoon and, when the dough starts coming together, turn it out onto a clean and dry worktop and knead gently by hand until smooth. The dough will be stiff and only slightly tacky. Wrap in cling film and let it rest in the fridge while you prepare the filling.

2. Finely crush the biscuits by hand in a bowl large enough to take all the ingredients. Add the cocoa, candied peel, raisins, hazelnuts and vanilla.

3. Put the quince paste and rum in a small microwave-safe bowl, and warm them in the microwave for about 40 seconds to soften the paste. Combine the paste and rum with a fork until homogeneous, then add to the biscuit mixture and mix thoroughly to form a firm paste. Lay a 40-cm (16-in) long sheet of cling film on the worktop, tip half of the paste onto it and shape it as a 30-cm (12-in) long sausage by rolling it on the cling film. Wrap it in the film and twist the ends. Repeat with the remaining paste to make a second wrapped sausage then chill them both in the freezer for at least 30 minutes.

4. When ready to bake, set the shelf in the middle of the oven and preheat it to 180°C/350°F/Gas mark 4. Line a baking sheet with baking paper or a silicone mat.

Recipe continues overleaf

PREP TIME: 50 minutes, plus resting and chilling

TOTAL BAKING TIME: 15–17 minutes

BAKING TEMPERATURE: 180°C/350°F/Gas mark 4

dairy-free, egg-free

For the coating
250g (9oz) dark chocolate chips, or bar broken into small pieces (50–55% cocoa solids)
1 tbsp vegetable oil (preferably corn or sunflower)

5. Divide the chilled dough into two halves. Set one half aside and roll the other to 5mm (¼in) thickness over a lightly floured, 35-cm (14-in) long sheet of baking paper. Shape the pastry as a rectangle, about 10 x 30cm (4 x 12in), and position it on the worktop with a long side facing you. Unwrap one of the sausages of filling and place it on the dough. Use the baking paper to lift the dough and wrap it around the filling, slightly overlapping the joint; press very gently on the overlap to seal it. Using the baking paper under the pastry, flip the whole log over so that the seal is on the underside. Flatten the log gently with the palm of your hand to about 3cm (1¼in) thickness.

6. Trim off the two ends to neaten them, then cut the log into 6 equal pieces, slicing at an angle so that each one is diamond shaped. Repeat the process to make a second batch of 6 biscuits, then arrange them over the lined tray. Bake for 15–17 minutes, or until they have slightly puffed up and the surface looks dry.

7. Leave the biscuits to cool on the baking sheet for 10 minutes, then transfer them to a wire rack to cool completely. I recommend leaving them to dry out for a few hours (or, better, overnight) before coating them with chocolate.

8. Put the chocolate and oil in a small bowl and microwave it for 1 minute, then stir well and keep microwaving in 10-second bursts, stirring it well between subsequent bursts until completely melted. Arrange the mostaccioli on a sheet of baking paper, then dip the tops in the melted chocolate. Allow the excess chocolate to drip back into the bowl then place the mostaccioli back on the baking paper to set. Mostaccioli keep for up to 2 weeks in an airtight container.

SWEET TREATS

Rocher	144
Mandorle pralinate	146
Datteri farciti	148
Arance candite	150
Capezzoli di Venere	154
Sbrisolona	156
Salame di cioccolato	158
Castagnaccio	160
Struffoli	162
Giurgiulena	165
Croccante	168

ROCHER

Meaning 'rock' in French, rocher became a synonym of elegant chocolate treats when Michele Ferrero, the same man who launched Nutella in 1964, invented the famous hazelnut pralines in 1979. Their production process is a heavily guarded secret and, to this day, only a handful of people know how they get coated in chocolate, yet remain perfectly round with no hint of a flat base forming while the chocolate sets...

My own version of rocher is certainly more accessible than Ferrero's and it produces equally delicious treats, infused with my top-favourite flavour combination: chocolate and hazelnuts. The optional layer of gold dust will turn your homemade rocher into a truly luxurious present, worthy of ambassadors and diplomats alike.

MAKES 12

100g (3½oz) Loacker Napolitaner wafers
100g (¾ cup) chopped toasted hazelnuts
100g (⅓ cup) chocolate and hazelnut spread
12 whole blanched and toasted hazelnuts
150g (5½oz) dark chocolate chips, or bar broken into small pieces (50–55% cocoa solids)
edible gold dust, to decorate (optional)

1. Crush the wafers by hand into small pieces, put them in a bowl large enough to accommodate all the ingredients and add half the chopped hazelnuts. Put the chocolate and hazelnut spread in a small microwave-safe bowl and microwave it just long enough to soften; 20 seconds should be enough. Add the softened spread to the wafer mix and combine. Chill in the fridge for at least 30 minutes.

2. Line a chopping board with baking paper. Once the mixture has cooled and looks firm enough to handle, divide it into 12 equal lumps, each about 20g (¾oz). Push a whole hazelnut in each lump, shape them as balls by rolling them between the palms of your hands then arrange them over the lined chopping board. This task is easier if you are wearing powder-free disposable gloves. Place the shaped pralines in the freezer to firm up for at least 15 minutes.

3. Meanwhile, melt the chocolate by microwaving it at full power for 1 minute. Stir well with a silicone spatula and, if bits of solid chocolate remain, give it subsequent 10-second bursts in the microwave, stirring well between bursts, until all the chocolate has melted. Add the remaining chopped hazelnuts to the chocolate and stir to combine. Drop each rocher in the chocolate mixture, one at a time, then lift it out with a fork, allow the excess chocolate to drip back in the bowl and return it to the lined chopping board to set.

4. For a touch of glamour, once the chocolate is set, drop the rocher, one at a time, in a small plastic bag, along with the tip of a teaspoon of gold dust. Hold the bag closed and shake it gently so the gold dust coats the rocher completely. Carefully transfer the coated rocher to a serving plate. Repeat with the rest, adding more gold dust to the bag as needed. Rocher are best stored in an airtight container and served at room temperature; they should be used within 1 week.

egg-free

PREP TIME: 25 minutes, plus resting and chilling

MANDORLE PRALINATE

Sugared almonds

You are guaranteed to smell the sweet and nutty scent of mandorle pralinate at every single town and village fair in Italy: this is the ultimate sweet treat, typically sold in paper cones or bags, that those celebrating the town's patron saint will nibble on while strolling in the central piazza.

My recipe includes cinnamon, vanilla and orange zest for added flavour, but even the basic version made with just almonds, sugar and water is on a par with much more elaborate desserts. And it takes no longer than 15 minutes to prepare!

I prefer to use blanched almonds, but unblanched ones are fine too. In fact, you can replace the almonds with the nuts of your choice: this method works perfectly well with pecan nuts, hazelnuts, cashews or, if you are feeling posh, macadamia nuts.

Mandorle pralinate are an excellent sweet treat on their own, but I often use them to decorate cakes or as a sophisticated topping for ice cream.

MAKES about 250g (9oz)

150g (generous 1 cup) whole blanched almonds
120g (²/₃ cup) caster (superfine) sugar
40g (8 tsp) water
1 tsp ground cinnamon
1 tsp vanilla bean paste
zest of 1 unwaxed organic orange

1. Line a wooden chopping board with a large sheet of baking paper.
2. Place all the ingredients in a frying pan; I find that stainless-steel pans are better when working with sugar, but a non-stick one would work just as well.
3. Mix everything together with a wooden spoon and bring to the boil over a medium heat, stirring the mixture constantly. The sugary solution will start bubbling and frothing, then, once the water has completely evaporated, it will look dry and sandy. At this point, lower the heat to the minimum and do not stop stirring: after a couple of minutes all the sandy sugar will have coated the almonds and they will start browning. Once the almonds have taken on a deep amber colour, remove from the heat and turn them out onto the lined chopping board. It will take less than 10 minutes in total to caramelize the nuts.
4. Use the spoon to break up the largest clumps and make sure you do not touch the nuts with your bare hands: they will be hot at this stage! Once they are cool enough to handle, break up any remaining clumps into individual almonds and leave to cool completely, although they are irresistible while still warm! Mandorle pralinate keep for up to 2 weeks in an airtight container.

Stuffed dates

One of the staples in my mother-in-law's repertoire, datteri farciti are a rich and sweet treat common across southern Italy and often prepared in the Christmas period. They are extremely simple to make and require no baking, yet the result is a decadent little nugget of sweetness, with a satisfying texture and a flavoursome filling.

They keep for long enough to be served to occasional guests during the festive season. For an alcohol-free version, omit the lemon zest and replace the limoncello with the same amount of strong espresso. If the amount of filling is too little for your food processor, double the quantities: leftovers can be rolled into balls and coated with melted chocolate to make delicious marzipan pralines.

MAKES 12

50g (scant ½ cup) whole blanched almonds
30g (2 tbsp) caster (superfine) sugar
1 tsp vanilla bean paste
zest of ½ unwaxed organic lemon
2 tsp limoncello
12 dates
80g (2¾oz) dark chocolate chips, or bar broken into small pieces (70–75% cocoa solids)

1. Put the almonds and sugar in the bowl of a food processor and blitz them to a coarse texture: you will need to scrape down the sides of the bowl a few times to process the small quantity. Transfer them to a small bowl and add vanilla, lemon zest and limoncello. Mix well with a spoon to make a firm paste. Cover the surface with cling film and chill in the fridge for at least 20 minutes.

2. Line a chopping board with baking paper. Cut a slit lengthways in the dates, pull out the stones and discard them. Shape a heaped teaspoonful of the almond paste as a small noodle, roughly the length of a date. Push the noodle of almond paste into the slit on a date and place it, slit side up, on the lined board. Repeat to stuff all the dates.

3. Put the chocolate in a small bowl and microwave it for 1 minute, then stir well and keep microwaving it in 10-second bursts, stirring well between subsequent bursts until fully melted. Set aside to cool for a few minutes. Drizzle the melted chocolate with a teaspoon across the stuffed dates, or pipe it using a small piping bag with a 3mm (⅛in) opening. Allow the chocolate to set. Datteri farciti keep for up to 2 weeks in an airtight container.

ARANCE CANDITE

Candied orange peel

Candied orange peel is recognized as one of the typically Italian flavours: it is arguably one of the most common ingredients in Italian bakes, and certainly represents the critical element of the coveted panettone flavour.

Chocolate-dipped orange peel was an unmissable element on the tray of festive biscuits that my dad use to prepare, in industrial quantities, every Christmas, and it added a much-needed splash of colour to the traditional selection of roccocò (page 136), susamelli (page 130) and mostaccioli (page 138).

The method for making candied peel might look daunting at first, but do not be put off, it really is super-easy and, most importantly, at almost zero cost! My recipe requires no skills whatsoever, just patience, time and good-quality oranges. Follow these steps for the best-tasting (and cheapest) candied peel you have ever tried. The peel can be used either as is, and added as an ingredient in future bakes, or turned into an original sweet treat with the addition of a decorative coating. I have used a coating of chocolate with coconut, hazelnuts, pistachios and – more extravagant – freeze-dried raspberries in this recipe, but you can pick whatever is available in your pantry.

I usually cut the peel by quartering the oranges, then slicing off the rind: this provides 4–5cm (about 2in) wide wedges that do not break up while cooking. This method can be scaled easily and works for however much peel you have, but I recommend going for larger batches, ideally 400–500g (14–18oz), and certainly never less than 200g (7oz).

MAKES about 700g (1lb 9oz), decorated

For the candied peel
200g (7oz) peel of unwaxed organic oranges, cut in 4–5-cm (about 2-in) wide strips
caster (superfine) sugar for the syrup, plus extra for coating

For the decoration (optional)
40g (½ cup) desiccated (shredded) coconut
70g (½ cup) chopped toasted hazelnuts
70g (½ cup) chopped unsalted pistachio kernels
15g (½ cup) freeze-dried raspberries
100g (3½oz) dairy-free dark chocolate chips, or bar broken into small pieces (70–75% cocoa solids)

1. On day 1, put the orange peel strips in a large bowl and cover them with fresh, cold water, then leave them to soak at room temperature for 24 hours. On day 2, drain and rinse the strips, cover them again with fresh, cold water and leave them to soak for a further 24 hours. These two initial soaks are not absolutely essential but they allow the bitter oils of the peel to leach out, producing a sweeter candied peel.

2. On day 3, drain and rinse the peel, place in a large pan, cover with fresh water and bring to the boil over a high heat. Simmer for 5 minutes, then drain and discard the cooking water, return the peel to the pan and repeat: cover with fresh water, bring to the boil, simmer for 5 minutes, then drain.

3. Weigh the boiled strips: the initial batch is likely to weigh 300g (10½oz) or more now, as it will have absorbed water during the soaking and cooking. Add the same weight (300g/10½oz in this example) in water and the same weight in sugar to a large pan, then bring to the boil over a high heat to make a syrup. When the syrup is boiling, add the drained peel, reduce the heat to low and simmer, uncovered, stirring often. Meanwhile, lay a large sheet of baking paper on a heatproof surface.

gluten-free, dairy-free, egg-free, vegan

PREP TIME: 1 hour over 4 days, plus soaking, cooking and drying time

4. The peel is cooked when it feels soft and looks translucent. By this time the cooking liquid in the pan will have reduced to just a few tablespoons of thick syrup; depending on quantities, this can take up to 1–1½ hours. Do not let the syrup dry out completely in the pan or the sugar will caramelize, producing very hard peel.

5. Take the pan off the heat and, using a fork or, better, a pair of tongs, pick out the strips one by one and place them in a single layer on the baking paper to cool and dry for at least 12 hours or, better still, for 24–48 hours.

6. Once the peel feels only slightly tacky to the touch, transfer the strips to a large bowl and sprinkle them generously with caster sugar: toss them to coat entirely so that the pieces do not stick together when stored. The candied orange peel can be stored for up to 2 months in an airtight container, ready to be diced, sliced or nibbled on.

7. If decorating, put the coconut, hazelnuts, pistachios and raspberries in separate bowls. Slice the candied peel into smaller strips, each about 8–10mm (⅜– ½in) wide, and lay a large sheet of baking paper on the worktop.

8. Melt the chocolate in a microwave-safe bowl by microwaving it on full power for 30 seconds. Stir well and, if bits of solid chocolate remain, give it subsequent 5-second bursts in the microwave, stirring well between bursts, until the chocolate is fully melted.

9. Dip a strip of peel into the chocolate, up to about a third of its length, then roll it in the dried nuts or fruit and leave it to set on the baking paper. Repeat with all the strips.

CAPEZZOLI DI VENERE

Venus's nipples

In the 1984 period drama *Amadeus*, capezzoli di Venere were described as 'quite surprising' and 'marvellous'. Apparently, the Italian composer Antonio Salieri, who is seen in the movie offering them to Mozart's wife, was a real fan of these chestnut and brandy truffles, so much so that he always brought generous stocks from his hometown Legnago (where they were created in the eighteenth century), to the Austrian capital, where they were appreciated at the Habsburg court.

Amadeus is not the only claim to fame of these cheeky delicacies, as they have also appeared in the romantic fantasy *Chocolat* and, more recently, in *Paris Can Wait*.

The recipe calls for cooked chestnuts: the pre-cooked ones sold in vacuum-sealed packets are the most convenient option, but you can also cook your own in boiling water for 1–2 hours. Chestnuts only add a subtle nutty flavour to the chocolate and cream core, but they produce the creamiest, most melt-in-the-mouth texture, perfectly washed down by a glass of sweet Marsala wine.

MAKES 16

100g (3½oz) dark chocolate drops (50–55% cocoa solids), plus extra to decorate
70g (¼ cup) whipping (heavy) cream (35–40% fat)
120g (about 1 cup) cooked chestnuts
2 tbsp brandy or dark rum
200g (7oz) white chocolate chips, or bar broken into small pieces

1. Put the dark chocolate drops in a medium bowl and set aside. Put the cream in a small saucepan and bring it to a gentle simmer over a medium heat. Once simmering, pour the cream over the chocolate, cover the bowl with a plate and leave it, undisturbed, for 3 minutes. Stir the mixture very gently until homogeneous, then cover it again and let it rest for a further 3 minutes.

2. Meanwhile, put the chestnuts in the bowl of a food processor and blitz them until they have the texture of fine sand. Add the ground chestnuts and brandy to the chocolate mixture and stir well to combine. Cover with cling film and chill in the fridge for at least 30 minutes.

3. Line a chopping board with baking paper and set aside. Once the mixture has cooled and looks firm enough to handle, take it out of the fridge and divide it into 16 equal lumps, each about 20g (¾in). Shape them as balls by rolling them between the palms of your hands, then arrange them over the lined chopping board. This task is easier if you are wearing powder-free disposable gloves. Flatten the truffles slightly, just enough to stop them from rolling away, then place them in the freezer to firm up for at least 15 minutes.

4. Meanwhile, melt the white chocolate by microwaving it at full power for 1 minute. Stir well with a silicone spatula and, if bits of solid chocolate remain, give it subsequent 10-second bursts in the microwave, stirring well between bursts, until the chocolate is fully melted. Drop each truffle in the melted chocolate, then lift it out with a fork, allow the excess chocolate to drip back in the bowl and return it to the lined chopping board to set. Before the chocolate sets completely, decorate the top of each truffle with a dark chocolate drop. Store in an airtight container in the fridge, but serve at room temperature and use within 1 week.

PREP TIME: 30 minutes, plus resting and chilling

gluten-free, egg-free

SBRISOLONA

Although referred to as a 'torta' in Italian, sbrisolona is closer to a biscuit than to a cake. The name comes from brisa, meaning crumble in the local dialect, and the end result does resemble the top layer of a traditional crumble dessert, albeit much crunchier and nuttier. Its birthplace is Mantua, although sbrisolona can be found in most of northern Italy.

The recipe is so rustic that you are not allowed to slice sbrisolona neatly: people from Mantua are adamant that it must be broken into pieces and enjoyed with bare hands. The small addition of lard provides an unbeatable crispness to the texture, and the cornmeal helps make it pleasantly coarse. Do avoid any polenta mixes that are pre-treated for quicker cooking: you must use raw, finely ground corn for this recipe.

A small bite of this crispy, sweet, biscuity cake goes very well with an after-lunch espresso or as a topping for a gelato, and it is simply unbeatable when dipped in vin santo or Marsala wine at the end of an indulgent dinner. It pairs very well with chocolate (page 173) or mascarpone sauce (page 175), or even drizzled with a generous helping of caramel sauce (page 181). It keeps for up to a couple of weeks, so it is a good option for a sweet present.

SERVES up to 14

for a 27cm (10¾in) tart or springform cake tin

170g (about 1½ cups) whole unblanched almonds

120g (generous ½ cup) demerara (light brown) sugar, plus 1 tbsp to decorate

120g (scant 1 cup) soft wheat 00 flour or plain (all-purpose) flour

90g (scant ⅔ cup) finely ground cornmeal

zest of 1 unwaxed organic lemon

1 tsp ground cinnamon

⅛ tsp salt

70g (⅓ cup) cold unsalted butter, diced, plus extra for greasing

50g (3½ tbsp) cold lard, diced

20g (¾oz) egg yolk (about 1 large egg yolk)

20g (4 tsp) amaretto liqueur

1. Set the shelf in the lowest position of the oven and preheat it to 170°C/340°F/Gas mark 3½. Grease the tin and line the base with baking paper.

2. Set aside about 30g (¼ cup) of whole almonds and blitz the rest with the sugar in a food processor on high speed for just a few seconds, or with 2–3 pulses, if the function is available. The almonds have to be just roughly chopped and not reduced to a powder: larger, bean-size pieces are perfectly acceptable.

3. Tip the almond mixture into a bowl large enough to accommodate all the ingredients, and add the flour, cornmeal, lemon zest, cinnamon and salt. Mix the dry ingredients together with a spoon until fully combined. Make a well in the middle of the mixture and add the butter, lard, egg yolk and amaretto. Start working the ingredients by pinching the pieces of butter and lard with your fingertips, to incorporate the dry ingredients gradually. Break up any large clumps until you have a mixture with the texture of a chunky crumble.

4. Scatter the crumbly dough into the prepared tin, keeping the crumbles loose and without compacting them down. Decorate the top by pushing the reserved whole almonds halfway into the dough and sprinkling over 1 tablespoon of sugar. Bake for 40–45 minutes until the edges just start to turn amber. For a crunchier bite, bake for 3–5 minutes longer. Allow to cool completely before taking out of the tin. Sbrisolona keeps for up to 2 weeks under a cake dome.

PREP TIME:
15 minutes

TOTAL BAKING TIME:
40–45 minutes

BAKING TEMPERATURE:
170°C/340°F/Gas mark 3½

SALAME DI CIOCCOLATO

Chocolate salami

An Italian staple of the seventies, the iconic salame di cioccolato is still a very popular treat today. As it is super-easy to make and requires no baking, it is the perfect venture to entertain the kids on a rainy afternoon. The basic recipe includes just Rich Tea biscuits, but it can be made with whatever you may have in your cupboard: it works extremely well with digestive biscuits (graham crackers) or, if you like the combination, with ginger nuts. I have enriched mine with toasted hazelnuts and pistachios, to give it extra crunch, but you can experiment with more exotic additions, such as dried apricots or, if you like it, crystallized ginger.

The original version uses raw eggs, but I have modified mine so the eggs are cooked at relatively low temperature in hot chocolate. Like real salami, it gets better with time, so prepare it one or two days in advance to savour it at its best. Kids love to nibble on a slice of salame di cioccolato as an afternoon snack, but it can be easily turned into an unusual and quirky end-of-meal dessert with a dollop of mascarpone sauce (page 175) or just a swirl of whipped cream.

For an alcohol-free version, replace the liqueur with freshly squeezed orange juice.

MAKES up to 12 slices

60g (2¼oz) egg (about 1 large egg)
40g (¼ cup) caster (superfine) sugar
1 tsp vanilla bean paste
⅛ tsp salt
90g (3¼oz) dark chocolate chips, or bar broken into small pieces (70–75% cocoa solids)
60g (2¼oz) milk chocolate chips, or bar broken into small pieces (30–35% cocoa solids)
30g (2 tbsp) unsalted butter
30g (2 tbsp) Strega liqueur or dark rum
60g (2¼oz) Rich Tea biscuits or other light, crisp sweet variety
30g (about ¼ cup) unsalted pistachios
30g (about ¼ cup) toasted chopped hazelnuts
about 50g (⅓ cup) icing (confectioner's) sugar, for dusting

1. Put the egg, sugar, vanilla and salt in a small bowl then beat lightly with a fork or a whisk just to combine the ingredients. Set aside.
2. Put the chocolate and butter in a heatproof bowl (preferably metal), large enough to accommodate all the ingredients. Place the bowl over a pan of gently simmering water, ensuring that the water does not reach the bottom of the bowl. Stir with a silicone spatula until the chocolate has completely melted and it has incorporated the butter. Lower the heat to the minimum and pour the egg mixture into the melted chocolate. Keep stirring continuously over a minimum heat for about 5 minutes. Remove from the heat, allow to cool for 5 minutes, then stir in the liqueur. Line the surface of the mixture with cling film and chill in the fridge for about 1 hour, or until the mixture has thickened up enough to be shaped.
3. Meanwhile, roughly break the biscuits by hand into chunks, more or less 2cm (¾in) each. Lay a large (about 40cm/16in square) sheet of baking paper on the worktop.
4. Take the chocolate mixture out of the fridge, add the broken biscuits, pistachios and hazelnuts, and stir gently until well combined. Turn out the mixture onto the baking paper and roll the sheet over the mixture to shape it into a large sausage, about 5cm (2in) thick and 25cm (10in) long, then secure it by twisting the ends of the paper.
5. Chill in the fridge for at least 5 hours, ideally overnight. When ready to serve, unwrap the salami and keep it on its baking paper. Dust it generously with icing sugar, roll it onto the baking paper and spread the sugar on it with your hands until thoroughly coated. Serve chilled, sliced on a chopping board. Salame di cioccolato keeps for up to a week in the fridge and can be frozen for up to a month.

PREP TIME:
20 minutes, plus cooling time and setting overnight

Chestnut squares

Castagnaccio is named after castagna, chestnut in Italian, the prime ingredient of this unusual dessert. Early written evidence of castagnaccio dates it back to sixteenth-century rural Tuscany, although it has now become a traditional autumnal bake of most of central and northern Italy, with a myriad of different names and local variations.

This is very much a love-it-or-hate-it kind of treat: with no glutinous flour, raising agent or eggs, the texture of castagnaccio is rather squishy, almost similar to cold polenta, so much so that I struggle to classify it as a cake… Because it has such a dense structure, I prefer to keep it thin, certainly less than 2cm (¾in). The key to achieve a soft, pleasant texture is to avoid overbaking castagnaccio: as soon as the skin looks dull and only slightly crackly, it is done.

Castagnaccio has no added sugar, and its flavour relies exclusively on the sweetness of the chestnut flour, so it is critical that this is of top quality and as fresh as possible. Ideally, castgnaccio should be baked in the autumn with chestnut flour ground the same year, as stale flour tends to taste bitter. You can certainly add a couple of tablespoons of sugar to the batter, but I prefer to bake the traditional recipe, and only add sweetness with a generous drizzle of chestnut honey on the plate. Pairing it with sweet wines like vin santo will not only keep it authentic, it will make a perfect match!

MAKES 24
for a 23 x 33cm (9 x 13in)
Swiss roll tin (jelly
roll pan)

3 tbsp extra virgin olive oil
80g (generous ½
 cup) raisins
60g (scant ½ cup)
 pine nuts
470g (3½ cups plus 1 tbsp)
 chestnut flour
¼ tsp salt
600g (2½ cups) cold water
80g (scant 1 cup) walnut
 pieces, chopped the
 size of a pea
2 tsp fresh rosemary
 leaves, stripped
 from stalks
3 tbsp chestnut honey
 or clear honey

1. Set the shelf in the lowest position of the oven and preheat it to 180°C/350°F/Gas mark 4. Brush the tin with 1 tablespoon of oil and set aside. Put the raisins in a small bowl, cover them with hot water and set aside to soak. Put the pine nuts in a small non-stick frying pan and toast them over a moderate heat, tossing them often until lightly golden.

2. Sift the flour into a bowl large enough to accommodate all the ingredients, add the salt and 1 tablespoon of oil. Place a damp tea towel (dish towel) under the bowl to stop it from moving then slowly trickle in the water while whisking energetically. Keep whisking until the batter looks smooth and lump-free: it will be rather liquid, almost like pancake batter. Drain the raisins and add half to the batter, along with half the walnuts and half the pine nuts. Whisk again to combine.

3. Pour the batter into the oiled tin and scatter the remaining raisins, walnuts and pine nuts on top, along with the rosemary leaves. Drizzle 1 tablespoon of oil over the surface and bake for no longer than 21–23 minutes, until the surface looks dull and slightly crackly, and springs back to the touch. Do not overbake or it will turn hard and rubbery. Leave it in the tin to cool down completely then transfer to a serving plate and cut into 24 squares with 5cm (2in) sides. Drizzle with honey just before serving. Without honey, castagnaccio keeps for up to 3 days covered with a tea towel or, in slices, in a biscuit tin.

PREP TIME: 15 minutes | **TOTAL BAKING TIME:** 21–23 minutes | **BAKING TEMPERATURE:** 180°C/350°F/Gas mark 4 | gluten-free, dairy-free, egg-free

STRUFFOLI

A glistening crown of struffoli, generously decorated with sprinkles and candied peels, is an unmissable element of the Christmas table in most of Campania. However, almost identical sweets, albeit with different names, are common across the whole of central and southern Italy.

Struffoli are fried balls of aniseed-flavoured dough, finished with a light coating of honey (the aniseed comes from the Italian liqueur sambuca). They are extremely simple to make, despite the rather tedious task of chopping the dough in a myriad of little balls. The original recipe calls for lard, which makes struffoli inherently dairy-free and unbelievably crispy, although unsalted butter could be used instead, if preferred. My family recipe includes a small addition of baking powder, which softens the dough just a little without compromising its crispiness.

To facilitate things, once fried, the little balls of dough can be stored in an airtight container for up to 2 weeks and coated with honey only when ready to serve. The crown arrangement is quite striking, but a simpler option would be to spoon the just-honeyed struffoli in single-portion ramekins instead.

SERVES up to 8

250g (1¾ cups plus 2 tbsp) soft wheat 00 flour or plain (all-purpose) flour, plus extra for dusting
½ tsp baking powder
20g (¾oz) caster (superfine) sugar
⅛ tsp salt
100g (3½oz) egg (about 2 medium eggs)
30g (2 tbsp) lard
50g (3 tbsp) sambuca, spiced rum or Cointreau
1 tsp vanilla bean paste
zest of 1 unwaxed organic lemon
sunflower or corn oil, for frying
peel of 1 unwaxed organic clementine, washed and dried
200g (¾ cup) clear honey
30g (1oz) candied orange peel (page 150), cut into thin strips
silver and gold sprinkles, to decorate

1. Sift the flour and baking powder into a bowl large enough to accommodate all the ingredients, add the sugar and salt, and mix with a spoon until fully combined. Make a well in the centre of the dry ingredients and add the eggs, lard, liqueur, vanilla and lemon zest. Combine the mixture with a spoon first, then start mixing by hand and, when the dough starts to come together, turn it onto a lightly floured worktop and knead until smooth. The dough will feel soft and slightly sticky. Wrap it in cling film and leave it to rest in the fridge for at least 1 hour. This will relax the dough and make the next step easier.

2. Take the rested dough out of the fridge and pat it down on a lightly floured worktop to shape it roughly as a square, about 2–3cm (about 1in) thick. Cut the square into 2–3cm (about 1in) wide slices, take one and roll it to form a thin noodle, no more than 1cm (½in) thick. Chop the noodle into little balls; they should be the size of chickpeas, then lift them up with a straight-edge scraper and drop them over a generously floured tea towel, tossing them around so that they get fully coated in flour and do not stick to each other. Repeat the rolling, chopping and flouring until you have used all the dough.

3. Set the fryer temperature at 180°C/350°F or use a pan large enough to comfortably fit the full batch of struffoli and fill it with at least 8–10cm (3–4in) of oil. Place the pan over a medium heat, controlling the temperature with a cooking thermometer. Line a tray with two layers of kitchen paper and position it next to the fryer.

Recipe continues overleaf

dairy-free, nut-free   **PREP TIME:** 45 minutes plus resting and frying time

4. When ready to fry, shake off the excess flour from the struffoli and carefully drop them into the hot oil. Fry until the dough turns deep golden, almost the colour of honey. It will take about 4 minutes: the longer you fry them for, the crisper they will be, but do not overdo it. Lift the fried struffoli out of the oil with a slotted spoon and drop them onto the lined tray.

5. Finely chop the clementine peel and set aside. Warm the honey in a medium saucepan over a medium heat until it just starts simmering, then drop in the fried struffoli and chopped clementine peel and stir to coat them thoroughly in honey. Place a cup, upside-down, in the centre of the serving plate and spoon the struffoli around the cup while the honey is still warm. Remove the cup only when the honey has cooled completely. Decorate the crown of struffoli with candied orange peel and sprinkles. Struffoli keep for up to 2 weeks at room temperature under a cake dome.

GIURGIULENA

Sesame and almond snaps

If you like Sesame Snaps, you will love giurgiulena: a traditional sesame seed and sugar candy made in Sicily and Calabria, typically at Christmas time, and often served on orange leaves.

The simplest recipes of giurgiulena call only for sugar, honey and sesame seeds, but I like to add almonds to balance the strong nuttiness of the sesame seeds, as well as candied orange peel (page 150) for a fresh and citrussy aftertaste. The result is a delectable sweet treat, adored by kids, but perfectly suitable also for the most discerning adult palate.

I am using a cheeky trick to dodge the usual complications that come with working with sugar: my recipe does not use any! Instead, it uses white fondant, making the whole process much easier and stress free.

Giurgiulena keeps for a long time, especially if stored away from moisture; this makes it a very popular treat to give as a Christmas present, together with mandorle pralinate (page 146) and croccante (page 168). This recipe can easily become vegan by swapping honey for glucose syrup.

MAKES about 300g (10½oz)

90g (3¼oz) white ready-to-roll fondant
80g (5 tbsp) clear honey or glucose (light corn) syrup
50g (5⅔ tbsp) sesame seeds
50g (⅔ cup) flaked (slivered) almonds
50g (1¾oz) candied orange peel (page 150), finely chopped

1. Line a wooden chopping board with a large sheet of baking paper and prepare a second sheet of baking paper, roughly the same size as the first.
2. Break the fondant into chunks and put it into a clean saucepan. Add the honey and place over a medium heat. Stir the mixture occasionally with a wooden spoon, until the fondant is completely melted.
3. Add the sesame seeds, almonds and orange peel and cook, stirring continuously, until the almonds look toasted and the mixture is a deep amber/caramel colour; it takes 5–10 minutes.
4. Pour the hot mixture onto the lined chopping board, cover it with the second sheet of baking paper and roll it as thin as possible with a rolling pin while it is still hot. The thinner you go, the crisper it will be.
5. Leave to set, then peel off the top sheet of baking paper and, while it is still warm, score it in a diamond pattern using a sharp knife. Once cool and brittle, break up the giurgliulena following the scored pattern. They keeps in an airtight container for up to a month: avoid using zip-lock bags as they tend to stick to the sugarwork. Giurgiulena is very sensitive to air moisture and it will become quite sticky very quickly in a humid atmosphere, so avoid storing it in the fridge.

PREP TIME: less than 15 minutes, plus cooling time

gluten-free, dairy-free, egg-free

CROCCANTE

Not many recipes have as few ingredients as croccante: in its classic form, it is made with just almonds and sugar in equal quantities. Some identify its birthplace in fifteenth-century Spain, others in thirteenth-century Italy, probably as a descendant of an even older Middle Eastern sweet based on nuts, sugar and honey. Whichever way you look at it, croccante boasts a rather impressive lineage, at least a few centuries old.

These days, it is an unmissable element of the many local fairs all over Italy, as well as being a favourite homemade treat to give as a thoughtful present over the festive season, as it keeps well for weeks, as long as it is well wrapped and kept away from moisture.

My family recipe has a couple of extra ingredients to produce a crisper caramel, easier to bite and less hard. Don't be put off making the caramel: it is much less daunting than it sounds. My only recommendation is to prepare everything in advance, both weighed ingredients and equipment, as timing is particularly important.

MAKES about 450g (1lb)

vegetable oil, preferably corn or sunflower, for greasing
250g (about 2 cups) whole blanched almonds or your favourite unsalted nut mix
60g (4 tbsp) clear honey
130g (½ cup plus 2 tbsp) caster (superfine) sugar
40g (3 tbsp) unsalted butter, at room temperature
⅛ tsp salt

1. Set the shelf in the middle of the oven and preheat it to 180°C/350°F/Gas mark 4. Line a wooden chopping board with a large sheet of baking paper and prepare a second sheet of baking paper, roughly the same size as the first. Grease them both with a few drops of vegetable oil and set aside.

2. Scatter the almonds over a baking tray and toast them for 10-12 minutes, shaking the tray midway to ensure an even baking. If you are using pre-toasted almonds, warm them up anyway in the oven for 3–5 minutes. Take the almonds out of the oven, cover them with a tea towel (dish towel) to keep them warm and set aside.

3. Put the honey in a microwave-safe bowl and warm it up until it just starts to simmer: 20–30 seconds in the microwave should suffice. Cover the bowl to keep it warm and set aside.

4. Tip the sugar into a saucepan, preferably stainless steel, big enough to accommodate the almonds too, then heat it gently over a moderate heat. The edges of the sugar will soon start to melt: at this point start stirring it gently with a wooden spoon.

5. As soon as all the sugar has melted and you see no residual white grains, add the hot honey, butter and salt to the mixture and keep stirring. The sugar will bubble and froth while the moisture evaporates.

6. Add the warm almonds to the caramel and mix thoroughly with the wooden spoon. Pour the mixture over the lined chopping board, cover it with the second sheet of baking paper (oiled face down) and roll it to about 1cm (½in) thickness. Do not be tempted to touch the mixture with your bare hands as it is extremely hot and dangerously sticky!

7. Once the croccante is set, chop it into small bars or squares with a sharp chef's knife: you might need to beat it down with the rolling pin. Croccante keeps for up to a month, wrapped in baking paper and in an airtight container. Avoid using zip-lock bags as they tend to stick to the sugarwork.

gluten-free/
egg-free

PREP TIME: 20 minutes,
plus cooling time

SAUCES

Salsa al cioccolato al latte	173
Salsa allo yogurt	173
Salsa al mascarpone	175
Salsa al cioccolato fondente	177
Salsa ai lamponi	179
Salsa alle fragole	180
Salsa al caffè	180
Salsa al caramello	181

SALSA AL CIOCCOLATO AL LATTE
Milk chocolate sauce

This milk chocolate sauce is a classic, smooth enough to go well with pretty much any cake without being overwhelmingly chocolatey or sickly sweet. It is an ideal dip for biscuits like krumiri (page 113) or frollini di riso (page 94) and it makes a perfect chocolate fondue. For a non-alcoholic version, swap the liqueur for the same amount of milk.

MAKES about 350g (12oz)

150g (5½oz) milk chocolate chips or bar
  (30–35% cocoa solids)
150g (¾ cup) whipping (heavy) cream (35–40% fat)
2 tbsp clear honey
1 tsp vanilla bean paste
2 tbsp Kahlúa liqueur or, for a stronger kick, vodka

1. If using a chocolate bar, chop it into small pieces with a sharp knife. Put the cream, honey and vanilla in a small saucepan then bring it to a gentle simmer over a medium heat. When the cream starts simmering, reduce the heat to the minimum, then add the chocolate and stir gently until it has fully dissolved. Remove from the heat and add the liqueur.
2. If not using immediately, pour the sauce into a sealed glass container and store it in the fridge: it will keep for up to 3 days. This sauce will firm up on cooling. However, it is at its best when served warm, so, before using, warm it in 10-second bursts in the microwave, stirring well between bursts, until the desired temperature is reached.

PREP TIME: less than 10 minutes

gluten-free, egg-free, nut-free

SALSA ALLO YOGURT
Yogurt sauce

Salsa allo yogurt is a fresh and delicately zingy sauce that takes less than 10 minutes to prepare. It goes particularly well with fruity cakes, and it is perfect to top a summery fruit salad. For extra sweetness, stir in a tablespoon of clear honey when adding the yogurt.

MAKES about 520g (1lb 3oz)

200g (¾ cup plus 1 tbsp) whipping (heavy) cream
  (35–40% fat)
80g (scant ½ cup) caster (superfine) sugar
2 tsp vanilla bean paste
230g (generous 1 cup) unsweetened natural (plain)
  yogurt (use whole, not low-fat)
zest of 1 unwaxed organic lemon or lime

1. Put the cream, sugar and vanilla in a medium bowl and whisk at high speed with a handheld electric whisk. Reduce the speed of the whisk when the cream starts to hold its shape and stop as soon as its surface turns from glossy to dull. Gently fold in the yogurt and the citrus zest. Salsa allo yogurt keeps for up to 2 days in the fridge and it is best served chilled. Give it a gentle stir just before serving.

PREP TIME: 5 minutes

gluten-free, egg-free, nut-free

SALSA AL MASCARPONE

Mascarpone sauce

Salsa al mascarpone is very rich, creamy and satisfyingly sweet. As well as being really easy to make, it is also extremely versatile: it pairs perfectly well with bold flavours, such as coffee in torta caffè corretto (page 28), or chocolate in torta ubriaca (page 36), but it complements equally well the more delicate flavours of fruity or citrussy cakes. For an alcohol-free version, swap the liqueur for the same amount of milk.

What I love the most about this sauce is that its consistency can be controlled quite easily: whisk it very gently to make a pourable sauce or whip it more energetically until the mixture starts to hold its shape to turn it into a stiffer, spoonable cream. This can then be either used to fill and coat traditional layered cakes, or served as a dessert on its own, scattered with strips of candied orange peel (page 150) and a light dusting of cocoa powder.

MAKES about 500g (1lb 2oz)

250g (generous 1 cup) mascarpone
130g (½ cup) whipping (heavy) cream (35–40% fat)
80g (⅔ cup) icing (confectioner's) sugar
2 tsp vanilla bean paste
zest of 1 unwaxed organic orange
2 tbsp sweet Marsala, Cointreau or Grand Marnier

1. Put the mascarpone, cream, icing sugar and vanilla in a medium bowl and mix the ingredients together with a spoon to break up the large clumps of mascarpone. Gently whisk by hand or use a handheld electric whisk at low speed, just long enough to combine all the ingredients into a smooth, pourable sauce.

2. Fold the orange zest and liqueur into the sauce and chill. Salsa al mascarpone keeps for up to 2 days in the fridge and it is best served chilled. Give it a gentle stir just before serving.

PREP TIME: 5 minutes

gluten-free, egg-free, nut-free

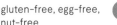

Dark chocolate sauce

This sauce is exclusively for true chocolate lovers: it is stronger than the milk chocolate sauce on page 173 and it pairs extremely well with vanilla-, coffee- or chocolate-flavoured cakes. Play with different flavours and try adding a pinch of chilli powder, salt, orange extract or black pepper. The method is foolproof: the process is specifically designed to avoid the risk of splitting, so you will end up with a perfectly smooth sauce every time. For a non-alcoholic version, simply omit the spirit.

MAKES about 350g (12oz)

120g (4¼oz) dark
chocolate chips or bar
(70–75% cocoa solids)
150g (¾ cup) whipping
(heavy) cream
(35–40% fat)
50g (¼ cup) caster
(superfine) sugar
1 tsp vanilla bean paste
2 tbsp dark rum, whisky
or brandy (optional)

1. If using a chocolate bar, chop it into small pieces with a sharp knife. Put the chocolate in a medium, heatproof bowl. Put the cream, sugar and vanilla in a small saucepan then bring it to a gentle simmer over a medium heat. When the cream starts simmering, pour it over the chocolate, cover the bowl with a lid or a plate and leave it, undisturbed, for 3 minutes.
2. Stir the mixture very gently with a spoon or whisks until homogeneous, then cover it again and let it rest for a further 3 minutes. Add the liqueur, if using, and stir to incorporate.
3. If not using immediately, pour the sauce into a sealed glass container and store it in the fridge: it will keep for up to 3 days. This sauce will firm up on cooling. However, it is at its best when served warm, so, before using, warm it in 10-second bursts in the microwave, stirring well between bursts, until the desired temperature is reached.

PREP TIME: less than
15 minutes

gluten-free, egg-free,
nut-free

Raspberry sauce

Salsa ai lamponi is a deliciously tangy sauce to complement any fruit or mildly flavoured cake. Try pairing it with a chocolate cake for a guaranteed success. Purists will demand straining it to remove the seeds, but I never bother. I recommend preparing batches of this sauce in the summer, when raspberries are reasonably priced and at their sweetest: you can freeze it in jars and thaw it when needed. Swap the liqueur for freshly squeezed orange juice for a non-alcoholic version.

MAKES about 400g (14oz)

300g (10½oz) raspberries
  (fresh or frozen)
80g (scant ½ cup) caster
  (superfine) sugar
1 tsp vanilla bean paste
3 tbsp water
2 tbsp Chambord
  (raspberry liqueur)

1. If using fresh raspberries, wash then drain them. Put them in a small saucepan, together with sugar, vanilla and water, then bring to a simmer over a medium heat. Once the fruit starts simmering, reduce the heat and let it cook, uncovered, for 3–4 minutes, until it has softened and breaks apart easily.
2. Remove from the heat and blitz with a hand-held blender until smooth. To remove the seeds, push the sauce through a sieve (strainer) with the back of a spoon. Finally, add the liqueur.
3. If not using immediately, pour the sauce into a clean dry jar, seal and leave to cool, then store it in the fridge and serve chilled. Salsa ai lamponi keeps in the fridge for up to 2 days.

PREP TIME:
less than 15 minutes

gluten-free, dairy-free,
egg-free, nut-free

SALSA AL CAFFÈ
Coffee sauce

Salsa al caffè is a perfect accompaniment for torta caffè corretto (page 28) but it goes equally well with mildly flavoured cakes like migliaccio (page 42). It is very easy to make, but make sure that the coffee is chilled before adding it to the whipped cream, as warmth would otherwise deflate it. Coffee liqueur (Kahlúa is the best-known brand) or sambuca is an essential element of this sauce, but for a non-alcoholic version, swap it for the same amount of espresso.

MAKES about 480g (about 1lb)

300g (1½ cups) whipping (heavy) cream (35–40% fat)
70g (scant ⅓ cup) caster (superfine) sugar
1 tsp vanilla bean paste
80g (about 5 tbsp) espresso, cold
2 tbsp Kahlúa or sambuca liqueur

1. Place 200g (1 cup) of cream, the sugar and vanilla in a medium bowl and whisk at high speed with a handheld electric whisk. Reduce the speed of the whisk when the cream starts holding its shape and stop as soon as its surface turns from glossy to dull.
2. Add the espresso and liqueur to the remaining cream, then pour the mixture into the whipped cream and gently fold it in. Salsa al caffè keeps for up to 2 days in the fridge and it is best served chilled. Give it a gentle stir just before serving.

PREP TIME: 5 minutes   gluten-free, egg-free, nut-free

SALSA ALLE FRAGOLE
Strawberry sauce

Salsa alle fragole has a nice balance of tanginess and sweetness which makes it a guaranteed kids' favourite. Like the raspberry sauce (page 179), it is cheaper to prepare in the summer, when there are plenty of juicy and sweet strawberries available at a reasonable price: you can freeze it in glass jars and use it in the colder months. For a non-alcoholic version, swap the liqueur for freshly squeezed orange juice.

MAKES about 350g (12oz)

350g (12oz) strawberries (fresh or frozen)
60g (⅓ cup) caster (superfine) sugar
3 tbsp freshly squeezed orange juice
1 tsp vanilla bean paste
2 tbsp Fragolino (wild strawberry liqueur) or Grand Marnier

1. If using fresh strawberries, wash then drain them and remove the stalks. Roughly chop the larger ones and place in a small saucepan, together with sugar, orange juice and vanilla. Bring to a simmer over a medium heat. Once the fruit starts simmering, reduce the heat and let it cook, uncovered, for 5–6 minutes, until it has softened.
2. Remove from the heat and blitz with a handheld blender until smooth, then add the liqueur.
3. If not using immediately, pour the sauce into a clean dry jar, seal and leave to cool, then store it in the fridge and serve chilled. Salsa alle fragole keeps in the fridge for up to 2 days.

PREP TIME:
10 minutes   gluten-free, egg-free, nut-free, dairy-free

SALSA AL CARAMELLO

<u>Caramel sauce</u>

Salsa al caramello is dense, thick and flavoursome. Those with a particularly sweet tooth would swear that anything can benefit from the addition of a drizzle or three of this rich sauce: yogurt, ice cream, biscuits, even muesli. However, for me, few things are better matched than caramel sauce and chocolate cake. The espresso will not give it a coffee flavour but rather it enhances the depth of the caramel. For a salted version, add half a teaspoon of salt flakes at the end.

MAKES about 280g (10oz)

180g (¾ cup cup) whipping (heavy) cream (35–40% fat)
150g (¾ cup) caster (superfine) sugar
20g (1½ tbsp) unsalted butter
1 tbsp espresso
½ tsp salt flakes (optional)

1. Put the cream in a small, microwave-safe, spouted jug and warm it in the microwave for about 1 minute.
2. Add the sugar to a small saucepan and place it over the lowest heat possible. When the edges start to melt, gently stir it with a wooden spoon. As soon as all the sugar has turned into an amber caramel with no whitish lumps of solid sugar left, take it off the heat.
3. Immediately trickle the warm cream into the caramel while continuously stirring. The caramel will foam and froth initially, but it will stop as you keep adding cream. Once all the cream has been incorporated, put the saucepan back over the heat for a further minute, then take it off again, add the butter, espresso and salt (if using), and stir well to combine.
4. If not using immediately, pour the sauce into a clean dry jar, seal and leave it to cool: it will firm up on cooling. However, this sauce is at its best when served warm, so, before using it, warm it in 20-second bursts in the microwave, stirring well between bursts, until the desired temperature is reached. Salsa al caramello keeps in the fridge for up to 2 weeks.

PREP TIME: 10 minutes

gluten-free, egg-free, nut-free

INDEX

A

abbracci 96–7
almonds
  almond biscuits 92–3
  carrot cupcakes 60–1
  cheeky coffee cake 28–9
  cherry crumble tart 54–5
  clementine and almond cookies
    120–1
  coffee nuts 126–7
  croccante 168–9
  date cake 50–1
  fig rolls 118–19
  honey cookies 130–1
  marzipan tartlets 76–7
  parrozzini 82–4
  pear and prune strudel 44–7
  roccocò 136–7
  stuffed dates 148–9
  sugared almonds 146–7
Amarena cherries in syrup 19
  Amarena cherry rolls 128–9
  coconut and Amarena cherry
    cakes 52–3
amaretti biscuits
  amaretti and coffee cheesecake
    48–9
amaretto liqueur
  parrozzini 82–4
  sbrisolona 156–7
apples
  cherry crumble tart 54–5
  gobeletti 74–5
  Grandma's apple cake 24–5
apricot jam
  apricot macaroons 122–3
  butter biscuits 134–5
  jammy walnuts 117
apricot kernels
  parrozzini 82–4
apricot macaroons 122–3
apricots (dried)
  rum cakes 72–3
arance candite 150–3

B

baci di dama 110–12
beetroot and chocolate cupcakes
  66–7
berries
  berries and ricotta cake 32–3
  fruit tartlets 85–7
biscotti al limone 104–5
biscotti all'amarena 128–9
biscotti noci e marmellata 116–17
black grape cake 26–7
brandy
  dark chocolate sauce 176–7
  pear and prune strudel 44–7
  Venus' nipples 154–5
bundt tins 10, 11
butter biscuits 134–5

C

cakelets 58–89
cakes 22–57
camille 60–1
candied peel
  candied orange peel 150–3
  mostaccioli 138–41
  rum cakes 72–3
  sunken ricotta cake 56–7
cantucci 92–3
capezzoli di Venere 154–5
caramel sauce 157, 181
carrots
  carrot cupcakes 60–1
castagnaccio 160–1
castagnotti 100–1
caster sugar 15, 16
cat's tongues 124–5
Chambord (raspberry liqueur) 179
cheeky coffee cake 28–9
cheesecake caffè e amaretti 48–9
cherries
  Amarena cherries in syrup 19
  Amarena cherry rolls 128–9
  coconut and Amarena cherry
    cakes 52–3

cherry crumble tart 54–5
cherries (dried)
  polenta biscuits 102–3
  rum cakes 72–3
cherries (glacé)
  butter biscuits 134–5
chestnut flour
  chestnut and chocolate cakelets
    70–1
  chestnut cookies 100–1
  chestnut squares 160–1
chestnut honey
  chestnut squares 160–1
chestnut squares 160–1
chestnuts
  Venus' nipples 154–5
chocolate
  beetroot and chocolate
    cupcakes 66–7
  butter biscuits 134–5
  candied orange peel 150–3
  chestnut and chocolate cakelets
    70–1
  chestnut cookies 100–1
  chocolate and pear cupcakes
    68–9
  chocolate salami 158–9
  drunk chocolate cake 36–7
  gianduja fondant 78–9
  lady's kisses 110–11
  milk chocolate sauce 173
  pistacchio biscuits 106–7
  polenta cakelets 80–1
  rocher 144–5
  Shrove Tuesday cake 42–3
  stuffed dates 148–9
  sunken ricotta cake 56–7
  Venus' nipples 154–5
chocolate eggs
  Easter cake 40–1
chocolate and hazelnut spread
  hazelnut biscuits 108–9
  rocher 144–5
chocolate salami 158–9

ciambellone di Pasqua 40–1
cinnamon
    pear and prune strudel 44–7
    sbrisolona 156–7
    Shrove Tuesday cake 42–3
    sticky fig cupcakes 64–5
    sugared almonds 146–7
citrus fruits
    unwaxed organic 16
    see also lemons; oranges
clementines
    clementine and almond cookies
        120–1
    roccocò 136–7
    struffoli 162–4
    upside-down clementine cake
        34–5
cloves
    pear and prune strudel 44–7
cocoa powder
    coffee nuts 126–7
    drunk chocolate cake 36–7
    gianduja fondant 78–9
    hugs 96–7
    milky slice 88–9
    mostaccioli 138–41
coconut
    candied orange peel 150–3
    coconut and Amarena cherry
        cakes 52–3
coffee
    amaretti and coffee cheesecake
        48–9
    caramel sauce 181
    cheeky coffee cake 28–9
    coffee nuts 126–7
    coffee sauce 42, 125, 180
coffee nuts 126–7
cognac
    pear and prune strudel 44–7
Cointreau
    mascarpone sauce 175, 185
    struffoli 162–4
cornmeal

polenta cakelets 80–1
crinkle biscuits 104–5
croccante 168–9
crostatine al marzapane 76–7
cuor di Sicilia 56–7
cuore morbido al gianduja 78–9
cup measurements 15

D
dark chocolate sauce 42, 113, 176–7
dates
    date cake 50–1
    stuffed dates 148–9
datteri farciti 148–9
drunk chocolate cake 36–7

E
Easter cake 40–1
egg sizes 16

F
fan ovens 12
fetta al latte 88–9
fig rolls 118–19
figs
    sticky fig cupcakes 64–5
flour, measuring 15
fondant
    sesame and almond snaps 165–7
Fragolino (wild strawberry liqueur) 180
frollini di riso 94–5, 113, 173
fruit tartlets 85–7

G
gianduja fondant 78–9
ginger
    pear and prune strudel 44–7
giurgiulena 165–7
glacé cherries
    butter biscuits 134–5
gobeletti 74–5
Grand Marnier
    mascarpone sauce 175, 185
Grandma's apple cake 24–5

grapes
    black grape cake 26–7
    fruit tartlets 85–7
Greek yoghurt
    berries and ricotta cake 32–3

H
hazelnuts
    candied orange peel 150–3
    chocolate salami 158–9
    gianduja fondant 78–9
    hazelnut biscuits 108–9
    lady's kisses 110–11
    mostaccioli 138–41
    rocher 144–5
honey
    chestnut squares 160–1
    clementine and almond cookies
        120–1
    croccante 168–9
    date cake 50–1
    drunk chocolate cake 36–7
    fruit tartlets 85–7
    honey cookies 130–1
    krumiri 113–16
    milk chocolate sauce 173
    milky slice 88–9
    mostaccioli 138–41
    roccocò 136–7
    sesame and almond snaps 165–7
    sticky fig cupcakes 64–5
    walnut cake 38–9
    yoghurt sauce 173
hugs 96–7

I
ingredients, weighing and measuring
    15–16

J
jammy walnuts 117

K
Kalhúa coffee liqueur

amaretti and coffee cheesecake
48–9
coffee sauce 180
milk chocolate sauce 173
kiwi
fruit tartlets 85–7
krumiri 113–16, 173

L
lady's kisses 110–11
Laocker Napolitaner wafers
rocher 144–5
lemons
almond biscuits 92–3
Amarena cherry rolls 128–9
berries and ricotta cake 32–3
black grape cake 26–7
cherry crumble tart 54–5
crinkle biscuits 104–5
Easter cake 40–1
fruit tartlets 85–7
gobeletti 74–5
marzipan tartlets 76–7
pear and prune strudel 44–7
rum cakes 72–3
sbrisolona 156–7
Shrove Tuesday cake 42–3
struffoli 162–4
walnut cake 38–9
yoghurt sauce 173
limoncello
stuffed dates 148–9
lingue di gatto 124–5

M
mandorle pralinate 146–7
mangoes
fruit tartlets 85–7
Marsala
mascarpone sauce 175, 185
sunken ricotta cake 56–7
walnut cake 38–9
marzipan tartlets 76–7
mascarpone

amaretti and coffee cheesecake
48–9
beetroot and chocolate
cupcakes 66–7
mascarpone sauce 85, 157, 158, 175
milky slice 88–9
peach loaf 30–1
measuring ingredients 15–16
microwaves 12
migliaccio 42–3
milk chocolate sauce 95, 113, 125, 173
milky slice 88–9
mint
peach loaf 30–1
mostaccioli 138–41, 150

N
nicciolantini 108–9
nidi di cocco all'albicocca 122–3

O
orange marmalade
carrot cupcakes 60–1
marzipan tartlets 76–7
oranges
almond biscuits 92–3
beetroot and chocolate
cupcakes 66–7
candied orange peel 150–3
carrot cupcakes 60–1
date cake 50–1
marzipan tartlets 76–7
mascarpone sauce 175, 185
mostaccioli 138–41
orange cupcakes 62–3
parrozzini 82–4
pine nut cookies 98–9
polenta cakelets 80–1
roccocò 136–7
sesame and almond snaps 165–7
Shrove Tuesday cake 42–3
sticky fig cupcakes 64–5
strawberry sauce 180
struffoli 162–4

sugared almonds 146–7
sunken ricotta cake 56–7
ovens 12

P
pan di pesca 30–1
parrozzini 82–4
pasticcini al caffè 126–7
pasticcini di frolla montata 134–5
peach jam
butter biscuits 134–5
Grandma's apple cake 24–5
peach loaf 30–1
peaches
peach loaf 30–1
pears
chocolate and pear cupcakes 68–9
pear and prune strudel 44–7
pine nuts
chestnut squares 160–1
pine nut cookies 98–9
pinolini 98–9
pistacchini 106–7
pistachios
butter biscuits 134–5
candied orange peel 150–3
chocolate salami 158–9
pistachio biscuits 106–7
pisto 12
drunk chocolate cake 36–7
honey cookies 130–1
mostaccioli 138–41
roccocò 136–7
pizzicotti al mandarino 120–1
plumcakes 72–3
polenta biscuits 102–3
polenta cakelets 80–1
prunes
pear and prune strudel 44–7

Q
quince paste
mostaccioli 138–41

R

raisins
   chestnut squares 160–1
   mostaccioli 138–41
   polenta biscuits 102–3
   walnut cake 38–9
raspberries
   candied orange peel 150–3
   raspberry sauce 179
red wine
   drunk chocolate cake 36–7
rice biscuits 94–5
Rich Tea biscuits
   Amarena cherry rolls 128–9
   chocolate salami 158–9
   mostaccioli 138–41
ricotta
   amaretti and coffee cheesecake
      48–9
   berries and ricotta cake 32–3
   Shrove Tuesday cake 42–3
   sunken ricotta cake 56–7
roccocò 136–7, 150
rocher 144–5
rosemary
   chestnut squares 160–1
rum
   Amarena cherry rolls 128–9
   cheeky coffee cake 28–9
   dark chocolate sauce 176–7
   mostaccioli 138–41
   rum cakes 72–3
   struffoli 162–4
   Venus' nipples 154–5

S

salame di cioccolato 158–9
salsa al caffè 42, 125, 180
salsa al caramello 181
salsa al cioccolato al latte 95, 113,
   125, 173
salsa al cioccolato fondente 42,
   113, 176–7
salsa al lamponi 179

salsa al mascarpone 85, 157, 158, 175
salsa alle fragole 180
salsa allo yoghurt 30, 35, 85, 173
Sambuca liqueur
   cheeky coffee cake 28–9
   coffee sauce 180
   parrozzini 82–4
   struffoli 162–4
sbriciolata alle ciliegie 54–5
sbrisolona 156–7
sesame and almond snaps 165–7
settembrini 118–19
Shrove Tuesday cake 42–3
skewer test 11
sprinkles
   Easter cake 40–1
sticky fig cupcakes 64–5
strawberry sauce 30, 35, 180
Strega liqueur
   chocolate salami 158–9
   Easter cake 40–1
   mostaccioli 138–41
strudel pere e prugne 44–7
struffoli 162–4
stuffed dates 148–9
sugar, measuring 15
sugared almonds 146–7
sultanas
   rum cakes 72–3
   walnut cake 38–9
sunken ricotta cake 56–7
susamelli 130–1, 150

T

tartellete all frutta 85–7
tinware 10, 11
torine castagne e cioccolato 70–1
torine cioccolato e pere 68–9
torta al mandarino 34–5
torta alle noci 38–9
torta all'uva nera 26–7
torta caffè corretto 28–9, 175, 180
torta cocco e Amarena 52–3
torta di datteri 50–1

torta di mele della nonna 24–5
torta frutti rossie e ricotta 32–3
torta ubriaca 36–7, 175
tortine ai fichi 64–5
tortine alla polenta 80–1
tortine all'arancia 62–3
tortine barbabietola e chioccolato
   66–7

U

upside-down clementine cake
   34–5

V

Venus' nipples 154–5
vodka
   milk chocolate sauce 173

W

walnuts
   chestnut squares 160–1
   coffee nuts 126–7
   date cake 50–1
   fig rolls 118–19
   jammy walnuts 117
   walnut cake 38–9
weighing ingredients 15–16
whisky
   dark chocolate sauce 176–7
white chocolate
   pistacchio biscuits 106–7
   pistachio biscuits 106–7
   Venus' nipples 154–5

Y

yoghurt
   black grape cake 26–7
   coconut and Amarena cherry
      cake 52–3
   peach loaf 30–1
   yoghurt sauce 30, 35, 85, 173

Z

zaleti 102–3

Gluten-free recipes

berries and ricotta cake 32–3
caramel sauce 181
castagnaccio 160–1
chestnut and chocolate cakelets 70–1
chestnut squares 160–1
chocolate salami 158–9
clementine and almond cookies 120–1
coffee sauce 180
croccante 168–9
dark chocolate sauce 176–7
date cake 50–1
frollini di riso 94–5
giurgiulena 165–7
mascarpone sauce 175
milk chocolate sauce 173
nidi di cocco all'albicocca 122–3
pasticcini al caffè 126–7
pizzicotti al mandarino 120–1
raspberry sauce 179
rice biscuits 94–5
salame di cioccolato 158–9
salsa al caffè 180
salsa al caramello 181
salsa al cioccolato al latte 173
salsa al cioccolato fondente 176–7
salsa al fragole 180
salsa al lamponi 179
salsa al mascarpone 175
salsa allo yoghurt 173
strawberry sauce 180
torta di datteri 50–1
torta frutti rossie e ricotta 32–3
tortine castagne e cioccolato 70–1
yoghurt sauce 173

Dairy-free recipes

almond biscuits 92–3
apricot macaroons 122–3
arance candite 150–3
camille 60–1

candied orange peel 150–2
cantucci 92–3
carrot cupcakes 60–1
castagnaccio 160–1
chestnut squares 160–1
chocolate salami 158–9
clementine and almond cookies 120–1
coffee nuts 126–7
datteri farciti 148–9
drunk chocolate cake 36–7
giurgiulena 165–7
honey cookies 130–1
mandorle pralinate 146–7
mostaccioli 138–41
nidi di cocco all'albicocca 122–3
pasticcini al caffè 126–7
pine nut cookies 98–9
pinolini 98–9
pizzicotti al mandarino 120–1
raspberry sauce 179
roccocò 136–7
salame di cioccolato 158–9
salsa alle fragole 180
salsa al lamponi 179
strawberry sauce 180
struffoli 162–4
stuffed dates 148–9
sugared almonds 146–7
susamelli 130–1
torta al mandarino 34–5
torta ubriaca 36–7
upside-down clementine cake 34–5

nut-free recipes

abbracci 96–7
beetroot and chocolate cupcakes 66–7
berries and ricotta cake 32–3
biscotti al limone 104–5
biscotti all'amarena 128–9
black grape cake 26–7
cat's tongues 124–5
chocolate and pear cupcakes 68–9

ciambellone di Pasqua 40–1

coconut and Amarena cherry cake 52–3

cuor di Sicilia 56–7

dark chocolate sauce 176–7

drunk chocolate cake 36–7

Easter cake 40–1

fetta al latte 88–9

frollini di riso 94–5

fruit tartlets 85–7

gobeletti 74–5

Grandma's apple cake 24–5

hugs 96–7

krumiri 113–16

lemon crinkle biscuits 104–5

lingue di gatto 124–5

mascarpone sauce 175

migliaccio 42–3

milk chocolate sauce 173

milky slice 88–9

orange cupcakes 62–3

pan di pesca 30–1

peach loaf 30–1

plumcakes 72–3

polenta biscuits 102–3

polenta cakelets 80–1

raspberry sauce 179

rice biscuits 94–5

rum cakes 72–3

salsa al caffè 180

salsa al caramello 181

salsa al cioccolato al latte 173

salsa al cioccolato fondente 176–7

salsa al lamponi 179

salsa al mascarpone 175

salsa alle fragole 180

salsa allo yoghurt 173

Shrove Tuesday cake 42–3

sticky fig cupcakes 64–5

strawberry sauce 180

struffoli 162–4

sunken ricotta cake 56–7

tartellete alla frutta 85–7

torta al mandarino 34–5

torta all'uva nera 26–7

torta cocco e Amarena 52–3

torta di mele della nonna 24–5

torta frutti rossie e ricotta 32–3

torta ubriaca 36–7

tortine ai fichi 64–5

tortine alla polenta 80–1

tortine all'arancia 62–3

tortine barbabietola e cioccolato 66–7

tortine cioccolato e pere 68–9

upside-down clementine cake 34–5

yoghurt sauce 173

zaleti 102–3

Egg-free recipes

arance candite 150–3

candied orange peel 150–3

capezzoli di Venere 154–5

caramel sauce 181

castagnaccio 160–1

chestnut squares 160–1

croccante 168–9

dark chocolate sauce 176–7

datteri farciti 148–9

giurgiulena 165–7

honey cookies 130–1

mandorle pralinate 146–7

mascarpone sauce 175

milk chocolate sauce 173

mostaccioli 138–41

raspberry sauce 179

rocher 144–5

roccocò 136–7

salsa al caffè 180

salsa al caramello 181

salsa al cioccolato al latte 173

salsa al cioccolato fondente 176–7

salsa al lamponi 179

salsa al mascarpone 175

salsa alle fragole 180

strawberry sauce 180

stuffed dates 148–9

sugared almonds 146–7

susamelli 130–1

yoghurt sauce 173

GRAZIE, AGAIN!

Most of the content of these pages comes from my dad's chaotically handwritten recipes. His heap of disorganized notes exudes the baking knowledge and experience captured in the decades he spent relentlessly whisking eggs and piping cream, for work and for pleasure. This book is as much his as it is mine.

My Italian connections, Viviana, Fabiola, Vincenzo, great-aunt Vera, and my mother-in-law Giuseppina came to the rescue again: this selection of recipes would not have been the same without their input and priceless advice.

Thanks to Vivienne and Sarah for not giving up on me, and to Sophie, Claire, Matt, Rachel, Troy, Emma, Marianne and the entire team at Quadrille for contributing with their remarkable talents and extraordinary creativity to the making of this book.

Last but not least, thanks to Claudio Lugli (www.claudioluglishirts.com) for their stunning and glamorous shirts: they succeeded in the almost-miraculous task of making me look well-dressed!

ABOUT THE AUTHOR

Born and bred in Italy, Giuseppe moved to the UK in his early 20s with the plan to stay only for six months... Twenty years, one PhD, one happy marriage and three UK-born sons down the line, Giuseppe has elected England as his adoptive homeland and proudly crowned himself a 'Britalian'.

An engineer and researcher by trade, Giuseppe grew up in a family of passionate bakers, where food was the prime topic of conversation. He inherited from his dad, a professional chef, the love for everything cooked or baked. Winning the Great British Bake Off in 2021 sparked off his ambition to share his family gastronomic knowledge far and wide.

After contributing to the show's cookbook *A Bake For All Seasons* in 2021, he published his own, *Giuseppe's Italian Bakes* in 2022.

Since becoming a full-time baker, Giuseppe has been dipping his toes in a variety of exciting activities, from writing regular columns for magazines and newspapers to hosting on-line baking classes on global platforms, from baking live on national channels to guest appearances on British and Italian TV. giuseppedellanno.com

Managing Director
Sarah Lavelle

Project Editor
Sophie Allen

Copy Editor
Stephanie Evans

Designer
Studio Polka

Photographer
Matt Russell

Food Stylist
Troy Willis

Props Stylist
Rachel Vere

Head of Production
Stephen Lang

Senior Production
Controller
Sabeena Atchia

First published in 2023 by Quadrille,
an imprint of Hardie Grant Publishing

Quadrille
52–54 Southwark Street
London SE1 1UN
quadrille.com

Text © Giuseppe Dell'Anno 2023
Photography © Matt Russell 2023
Design © Quadrille 2023

Cataloguing in Publication Data: a catalogue record
for this book is available from
the British Library.

ISBN 978 1 78713 985 5

Printed in China

MIX
Paper | Supporting
responsible forestry
FSC™ C020056
FSC
www.fsc.org